The New Tarot

Sybil's
Smoke

She
Said:
Storm.

Sage
t
h
i
v
a
n
a
n
d
a
Sees Sleeping Soul's Struggle

Frontispiece: poem Tarot card, created by Edith F. Katz, using blank card from New Amazon Tarot

The New Tarot

Rachel Pollack

The Aquarian Press
An Imprint of HarperCollins*Publishers*

The Aquarian Press
An Imprint of Grafton Books
A Division of HarperCollins*Publishers*
77-85 Fulham Palace Road,
Hammersmith, London W6 8JB

First published by The Aquarian Press 1989

This paperback edition 1991

10 9 8 7 6 5 4 3 2 1

Rachel Pollack asserts the moral right to be
identified as the author of this work

British Library Cataloguing in Publication Data

Pollack, Rachel
The new tarot: modern variations of ancient
images.
1. Tarot cards. Designs, history
I. Title
133.32424

ISBN 1-85538-058-7

Printed in Great Britain by
Bath Press, Bath, Avon

Dedicated to Ingrid Toth

Contents

INTRODUCTION
The Re-Imagined Tarot

At one time the Tarot was a very specialized subject, a fascination to historians of playing cards, to occultists who saw it as an expression of secret wisdom, and fortune-tellers who used the pictures to predict tall, dark strangers and unexpected inheritances. Tarot decks tended to look alike, with their medieval scenes, their flowering sticks, and shiny discs. In fact, very few were available, and these were the standard ones that had been around for many years.

In the past ten or fifteen years this situation has changed dramatically. Not only have scores of new decks appeared, with more in preparation all the time, but the Tarot has also opened out, taking on new purposes, new concepts, above all new images, with a range of styles as various as the many decks' creators. There are Tarots based on other cultures, from Romany to Tibetan to ancient Mayan. There are Tarots which express the ideals and concepts of feminist spirituality. Major artists, including Salvador Dali, have produced Tarot decks. There is even a Tarot garden, with massive statues by the sculptress Niki de St Phalle. While most Tarot designers still seek a single deck to express perfectly their ideas, a number of others see their work as the production of Tarots, rather than *a* Tarot. In producing a series of decks, such people as Osvaldo Menegazzi, Guido Gillabel, or Elisabetta Cassari, revive a practise which flourished in earlier centuries.

Some decks aim at the commercial market, with easy-to-understand pictures, and a booklet instructing the reader on how to tell fortunes. Others seek to express an esoteric or psychological system. Still others present images of ancient Goddesses, or else they recreate a particular artistic style, such as the Ukiyoe period of Japan. Some decks are sold in ordinary bookshops as well as occult speciality stores. Others appear only in limited editions, each copy photographed or even hand-drawn by a dedicated artist.

This book attempts to explore some of these trends. The more than seventy decks shown here represent a wide sampling of the new areas where people have taken the Tarot, primarily in the past decade. While I have not included every deck published in this time, I have attempted to show the kinds of work people are doing, and the ways they have influenced each other. There are seven sections in the book: Art, Popular, Story-telling, Cultural, Women, Psychological, and Esoteric. The categories are not hard and fast. Several Art Tarots could easily fit with the Esoteric decks. The Merlin Tarot could move from Story-telling to Cultural or Esoteric, while the Norse, a Cultural deck, would fit very well with Story-telling. I have chosen these categories primarily to give form to the great variety of decks. One theme runs through them all, what I call re-imagining.

Occultists used to argue about the 'correct' Tarot. If Tarot images signified universal truths, then a particular set of images should exist which would embody these truths. The first people to look at the Tarot in this way, in the eighteenth and nineteenth centuries, stayed close to the conventional designs found on playing cards used in France and Italy and other places for the game of 'les Tarots'. When they made changes they sometimes claimed they were revealing the genuine pictures, long hidden from the public but passed down secretly from one generation to the next. Today we still find artists who will describe their decks as the one, perfected truth. However, even these tend to argue that they have received their information in meditation rather than from secret traditions. And the great majority of artists no longer insist on the absoluteness of their work.

Instead of diminishing that work, acceptance of individuality has given the artists a greater freedom. Some remain close to traditional design while varying them in small but highly individual ways. Others marry the conventional images to some particular style or concept. Still others choose entirely new pictures to express traditional themes. Some keep conventional titles for their cards. Others alter the names as well as the pictures, especially the court cards. The usual King, Queen, Knight, and Page have become King, Queen, Prince, and Princess, or Master, Companion, Amazon, Child, or Mother, Father, Daughter, Son, or Matriarch, Chief, Brave, Maiden.

Previously, people saw the Tarot as the expression of a particular philosophy, that of Hermetic occultism (see p. 136). Today, artists and designers have taken the freedom to adapt the Tarot to different religions, to psychological growth and transformation, to explorations of myth and dreams, to storytelling from fairy tales to *The Divine Comedy* of Dante Alighieri. They can do this because the Tarot consists of images rather than a fixed text. By changing the images we open up new possibilities. Previously, people sought a precise form to signify a precise idea. This approach certainly remains. However, the ideas themselves have widened out. And more and more people are playing with the images, discovering where their own pictures can take them.

Many people have put forth theories of the Tarot's origin. We will encounter a number of these in this book, including Chaldean astrology, ancient matriarchy, and Celtic initiations. Historically, the first known Tarot cards date from the early fifteenth century in Italy. From the beginning the deck consisted of seventy-eight cards, twenty-two trumps now known as the Major Arcana, and four suits, together called the Minor Arcana. The trumps quickly acquired names and a numbered sequence. In traditional decks the Major Arcana runs as follows:

0	Fool
I	Magician, or Juggler
II	Papess, or High Priestess
III	Empress
IV	Emperor
V	Pope, or Hierophant, or High Priest
VI	Lover(s)
VII	Chariot
VIII	Justice (in some decks, Strength)
IX	Hermit
X	Wheel of Fortune
XI	Strength (in some decks, Justice)
XII	Hanged Man
XIII	Death
XIV	Temperance
XV	Devil
XVI	Tower, or House of God
XVII	Star
XVIII	Moon
XIX	Sun
XX	Judgement
XXI	World

The Minor Arcana consists of Wands (or Staves or Batons), Cups, Swords, and Coins (or Discs or Pentacles). Each suit contains Ace through Ten plus four court cards (though some modern decks have reduced the court cards to three, as in ordinary playing cards). For a long time people saw the Tarot as an enjoyable game. Part of the enjoyment, however, must have lain in the mysterious images. Why did one card show a man hanging upside down with a radiant look on his face? Why a female pope? Why did the card of the Moon show a dog and a wolf howling before two dark towers, with a crayfish crawling out of a pool of water?

At the end of the eighteenth century a

man named Antoine Court de Gebelin made a startling claim. The Tarot, he wrote, formed an ancient Egyptian book of all wisdom, the Book of Thoth, created by the Egyptian God of magic, writing, medicine, and secret wisdom. (The Greeks and Romans saw Thoth as the equivalent of their own Hermes/Mercury. The term 'Hermetic' for European magic derives from Hermes Trismegistus, a legendary magician.) Court de Gebelin's idea caught on, especially when a man calling himself Etteila (his first name spelled backwards) produced an elegant Tarot, using mystical images.

In his work Court de Gebelin pointed to a fascinating correspondence. Since the Renaissance the two major influences on esoteric concepts in Europe had been (and still are) alchemy and the Jewish mystical tradition known as Kabbalah. The Kabbalah bases its mystic meditations on the twenty-two letters of the Hebrew alphabet. There are twenty-two trumps in the Major Arcana of the Tarot. The Kabbalah describes four worlds of creation, corresponding to the four medieval elements of Fire, Water, Air, and Earth. The Minor Arcana consists of four suits. The central image in the Kabbalah is the Tree of Life, a diagram linking ten 'sephiroth' (see p. 143, the Tree of Life Tarot). Each suit contains ten numbered cards.

In the nineteenth century Eliphas Lévi (Alphonse Louis Constant) formulated the Kabbalist Tarot. He assigned a particular Hebrew letter to each card, thereby placing the cards on the 'pathways' of the Tree of Life. Lévi's system still attracts followers, with many contemporary decks using his example of placing the Fool between cards XX and XXI. During this period occultism was going through a period of great popularity, so that the Tarot became more and more identified with Kabbalah.

One hundred years before the writing of this book, in 1888, MacGregor Mathers and others founded a new occult society, the Hermetic Order of the Golden Dawn. Though the Golden Dawn lasted only fifteen years, its influence on Tarot, ritual, and other esoteric matters, remains strong even today. Mathers altered and expanded Lévi's ideas, linking the Tarot to astrology and a system of meditations.

The Golden Dawn instructed its members to paint their own decks. Though it expected them to copy that of Mathers, some of them later went on to produce altered versions. For if Mathers had 'corrected' the traditional Tarot, why shouldn't they correct Mathers? One of those former Golden Dawn members was Arthur Edward Waite. In the beginning of the twentieth century Waite worked with an artist named Pamela Colman Smith to create a new Tarot deck. Nicknamed the Rider pack (the name of its London publisher), the Waite-Smith deck has become the most popular Tarot deck in the world. Not only are there editions in many languages and even different sizes, but also many subsequent decks have based their designs on those of Smith. In a number of the decks in this book we will find traces of the Rider pack, primarily in the Minor Arcana.

We could describe the Rider pack as the first re-imagined Tarot. First of all, Waite, like Mathers before him, created new concepts for a number of the trumps. More important (at least in terms of influence on later decks), Smith completely changed the Minor Arcana. Previous decks (and many later ones) show only a pattern of 'pips' on the numbered cards. That is, the Eight of Cups presents eight Cups arranged in some particular form. Smith's Minor Arcana contains a scene on every card. The Eight of Cups, for instance, shows a man walking up a hill in moonlight.

While some people have attacked this practice as a 'perversion' of occult principles, others have seen it as a liberation from fixed formulas of interpretation. We might also describe the Rider pack as the first story-telling Tarot. Some people see each suit as the story of the family shown in the court cards. We can also shuffle the whole deck, choose a few cards at random, and invent a new tale by linking the pictures together.

We cannot leave this capsule history of Tarot influences without mentioning one other name, that of Stuart Kaplan. The president of U.S. Games Systems Inc. probably has done more than anyone to popularize the Tarot, and to give unknown artists the chance to express their ideas. We will encounter Kaplan quite often in this book, for he has written the accompanying booklets for many of the decks. In his various instructions Kaplan not only displays a knowledge of subjects from ancient Egyptian society to Chaldean astrology, he also shows a flair for story-telling, spinning off possible events and legends from individual pictures.

The Tarot has always drawn untutored artists as well as professionals. Today as well the art ranges through all levels, from the most naive to the most complex. I have done my best to judge each deck on its own merits.

We can hardly compare the 'primitive' style of the Basque Mythical Tarot to the sophisticated technique of Salvador Dali. We can, however, attempt to discern whether an artist has approached the work with originality and vision. Unavoidably, the comments, even the choices, will betray my own biases. For mistakes and misinterpretations, as well as my own blind spots, I apologize. I apologize also for omitting any deck others might think of as vital to the Tarot's contemporary development. As mentioned above, this study is far from exhaustive. The excitement of the Tarot lies in its constant unfolding.

CHAPTER 1
Art Tarots

In its long history the Tarot has attracted surprisingly little interest from academic artists. While the earliest decks were often created by accomplished painters, such as the famous 'Visconti' Tarot of Bonifacio Bembo, the most renowned artists still tended to ignore the Tarot. Since then, many decks have been drawn by people with little training or knowledge of artistic traditions. These certainly possess their own power, especially when done with conviction and self-knowledge. A number of the decks shown here, such as the Omaha Old Market Tarot, take a deliberately 'naive' approach, as if recognizing the Tarot's history as a kind of folk art. Nevertheless, it seems strange that more classically trained painters have not responded to the opportunities in these magical images.

This situation has begun to change. A number of artists have created highly individual and sophisticated decks. Of more established figures, the legendary surrealist Salvador Dali has produced a Tarot that blends the conventional forms with scenes and figures borrowed from the history of art, the two held together by Dali's own language of symbolism and dream imagery. And in Tuscany, Italy, the sculptress Niki de St Phalle has created an astonishing Tarot garden, with statues towering over the trees, and one of them even serving as her home.

Different artists take very different approaches. Some, like Dali, will work closely with traditional images. Others, such as Hermann Haindl, have worked with the

Tarot ideas while re-imagining the entire deck. Or else, like Andrea Picino, have modernized the trumps, by setting explicit sexual images in geometric patterns. At different levels most of these artists accept the Tarot's esoteric traditions. Both Picino and Haindl see themselves as working with objective symbols of spiritual truth. The Tarot de Louttre breaks the standard images down to their fundamental forms. M. Louttre B. expresses these essentials with charm and wit. At the same time he clearly acknowledges a reality in those basic signs. This reality of meaning gives weight to the pictures. Even the idiosyncratic Tarots of Osvaldo Menegazzi work from an assumption that the Tarot can liberate us from spiritual oppression.

Many of the artists working with the Tarot have produced only small editions, with little distribution. This has made them difficult to find. The decks shown here represent only a sampling of the work being produced in many countries. As with all the categories in this book the selection is my own, made without hard criteria. I might easily have included the wonderful and unique Tarot Maddoni (from the Popular section), the Tarots of Elisabetta Cassari and the Minotarot (both from Story-telling and both from accomplished artists), and the stunning Voyager Tarot (Psychological). On the other side, the Haindl deck might have gone with the Esoteric Tarots, while at least some of Menegazzi's decks could belong in the Cultural section. In general, I have included in this section decks where the creator saw the work of art as the primary focus.

It is no accident that Italian decks dominate the selection. Along with Picino and Menegazzi, there are three decks published by Vito Arienti of Milan. And even though Niki de St Phalle is French American, her garden lies in Italy. The earliest – and some of the finest – decks came from Italy. As well as the Visconti decks (honoured by one of the Arienti publications), we find the Tarot Mantegna, and the Minchiate Tarots of Florence. Both Menegazzi and Arienti have published reprints of decks from their private collections. Throughout the centuries Italy and France (and southern Europe in general) have kept alive the tradition of Tarot as art. It is also no accident that in these places people played Tarot as a game, for there the cards remained alive and popular until that moment some two hundred years ago when occultists discovered (or rediscovered) the Tarot as a key to esoteric teachings. Happily that artistic tradition has begun to flourish again, perhaps as never before, in Italy and around the world.

Tarot De Louttre

On 24 October 1981 the Musée des Arts Decoratifs in Paris opened an exhibition titled 'cartes à jouer ançiennes, un rêve de collectionneurs'. As part of the exhibition they commissioned this highly original Tarot deck from M. Louttre B. The style of this deck is impressionistic, deliberately rough, with a sense of incompleteness, the picture seeming to emerge half finished. This rough quality begins with the back of the cards. Sharp lines move across a harsh surface like a torn piece of paper. Smudges and spots of ink take away any semblance of a polished work. In the bottom triangle the lines at upper left fail to meet, while some of the vertical lines either do not reach the angled lines or slip past the edge. The figure – two triangles meeting at the point – is an esoteric symbol, related to the six-pointed star, and signifying the meeting of polarities. It appears as well on the Four of Cups.

The deck, however, is not occult, at least not in the sense of a developed language of symbolism. It characteristically reduces any particular card to its essentials, which it then presents in a crude, almost childlike way. For the Papess we see only the hat and the book, for the Empress the orb with the cross, and a wonderful stick-figure bird (many traditional Empresses carry a shield displaying an eagle). For the Lovers we find a cliché heart pierced by an arrow. Crossed sprigs of gold above it give a more gentle quality. Force (Strength) gives us a witty image of barbells, with four red circles, smudged or broken. Notice that the crossed barbells again form the image of triangles joined at the point and that the three weights at each end resemble a Christian triple cross. More important, perhaps, the horizontal and angled lines give a sense of the card's fundamental meaning.

The card of Justice follows this same method, showing only the scales and the sword. Here again, however, we find symbolic implications in the forms. The scales hang suspended from an eye, symbol of intelligence and honesty. The wires of the scales form upward-pointing gold pyramids (gold is the alchemical symbol of realization),

while a downward-pointing triangle with green dots (the colour of new life) balances the polarity. Above the scales, the sword signifies the mental attribute of discrimination.

The sparseness in the deck makes the details constantly suggestive. In Temperance what does it mean that the jug and cup are upside down? In the Devil we see a smoky arrow coiled like a snake around a cliché pitchfork. The image suggests as well the healing wand of Aesculapius. Five flames hint at an upside-down pentacle, the classic symbol for the devil; but the prongs of the pitchfork form a sixth point. On the Fool faint lines beneath the crown hint at a tornado, the Fool's dance of ecstasy.

The symbols for the suits are as simple, and suggestive, as the Trumps. The Ace of Wands is a graceful tree, with soft leaves and yellow fruit. On the Three of Coins, the spokes on the wheels are all out of order, as if drawn by a child. The angled lines give a sense of the wheels rolling downhill. The Ace of Swords is blunt, without subtlety. Smudges, and even fingerprints, cover the two stars.

In the court cards the imagination of Louttre B. emerges in elegance and wit. The Knight of Wands appears as an outline of a face, with a fruit for an eye. The Queens all show a pair of eyes. For Cups we see these eyes in a spotted veil above the cup. The King of Swords shows simply an elegant dueling sword under a curlicued crown. Both sword and crown have that unfinished quality. For the Cavalier of Coins we see a spotted horse over a wheel.

In its deliberate crudeness the Tarot de Louttre creates an opposite pole from so many modern Tarots, with their emphasis on complexity. And yet, those crude and amusing images can lead us into subtle meanings.

Omaha Old Market Tarot

The Omaha Old Market Tarot, created by Sam Mercer, uses another kind of simplicity, that of standard Tarot images done in a style deliberately quick, as if by a somewhat older child than the one conjured up in Tarot de Louttre. The twenty-two pictures are soft, even delicate in their forms, with bright colours. The stick-like figures have a warm expressiveness.

The titles of the cards are in French, possibly

due to inspiration by the Tarot de Marseilles (my copy of the deck has no accompanying text). When we look closely we find a great number of subtle, often comical details. (*My awareness of the humour in this deck comes partly from the unusual way I first encountered it. I had gone to Italy to meet Niki de St Phalle and photograph her Tarot garden (see p. 32). Niki gave me an extra set she had of the Omaha Tarot. Shortly afterward she played a twenty-minute tape of people laughing and invited me to join her in laughing along with it, a spiritual and physical exercise programme which once*

helped her overcome a severe illness. She put on the tape, and while we were all laughing, I studied the Omaha Tarot.)

On the Fool the dog biting the leg is a trained puppy, standing on its hind legs and wearing a red sweater. In the corner stands a stick-figure crocodile, a hint of influence

from those modern decks which use Egyptian imagery. The Papess wears an absurd veil, looking almost like a beard. The poles on the card are crude lines, while at bottom right, what looks like folds of her dress is actually a misshapen creature with a smeared face.

The Lovers creates a carnival scene from

the theme of choice. The blonde woman, traditionally a symbol of purity, wears a dragon mask. The darker woman appears in a severe uniform, holding a shepherd's crook. The jester-like man rides a unicycle, as if to symbolize unity of purpose. But he wears a two-headed mask, with both faces grotesque. The Devil too suggests a carnival, or Hallowe'en, with a mask over his face. The Devil radiates waves of colour. In Strength the woman does not simply hold open the

lion's mouth, but has flipped the lion over and shackled its legs. The lion ends up looking like a kitten waiting to have its belly scratched.

As in a number of contemporary decks the Tower shows the downfall of urban civilization, with a vivid fireball and a slight hint of a mushroom cloud. The tower at the left has a café at the bottom. In the Moon we find dragon-like dogs and a brick road that spirals into the sky like a tornado in reverse.

Dali Universal Tarot

Like the Omaha Tarot the Salvador Dali deck often uses rough, smeared images. However, the great surrealist sets these against more sophisticated forms, very often pictures taken from the history of art. In the Hanged Man, the man comes from Nicholas Hilliard's *Young Man Among Roses*. The leaves above him are rough strokes of paint which drip down on to his legs. Beside him runs a smear. In the Moon, the claw of the crayfish reaches up like a great claw over the city, reminding us of primitive terrors deep within the lights and comforts of modern life.

The Dali Tarot is one of the two decks for which I have written a commentary (the other is the Haindl Tarot, see p. 28. I have also written a brief introduction for the Kashmir Tarot, described in the section on

Cultural Tarots.) Dali has chosen not to comment on the cards, so that my knowledge of the deck comes from my own study.

The use of the Hilliard painting is charac-

teristic of the deck, both in the contrast of images and in the use of a pictorial quotation. The cards unite the Tarot tradition with the history of art, and thus culture. The quotations are well chosen, as in the Hanged Man. The posture of Hilliard's figure almost exactly matches the classic form of the Hanged Man. In the Minor cards the quotations expand and inform the Tarot designs, the latter usually taken from Pamela Smith and the Rider pack.

The Three of Swords has Smith's pierced heart, but within it we see Perseus rescuing Andromeda, giving the theme of sorrow an undertone of courage through identification with mythological triumph. Interestingly, this exact scene – Perseus and Andromeda – appears in the Golden Dawn Tarot as the card of the Lovers. Dali's Four of Swords uses David's *Assassination of Marat* to paradoy

Smith's death-like knight within a church. Notice again the crude figure, which I have termed an 'ectoplasm'. These ghost-like images often undercut the central message. Here the snake suggests various possibilities, including the idea of evil from Marat's idealistic pen. In the Three of Wands, a successful burgher stands before one of his ships. He looks, however, at a ghost nude, perhaps symbolizing the lure of the dream world as well as sexual temptation. The butterflies covering the man are a recurrent motif in the deck, often obscuring the pictures.

Another recurrent image is the crutch, a motif which has long figured in Dali's paintings. He has written in the past that it signifies duality, a basic Tarot theme. In the Tower the crutch opens a kind of window into another reality.

The artist himself appears on two cards. In the Magician he stares out at us, while flames rise in the church behind him. On a box lie a broken loaf of bread, a glass of wine (the Christian communion), a rolled up scroll (a symbol we find in many decks on the High Priestess), and Dali's famous melting watch. The stare gives the Magician a comical air, a quality we find as well in the sleeping King of Pentacles, smudged over with fingerprints. In a gold cloud rising from his head we see him dreaming of a bull, symbol of Taurus, and Pentacles' element of Earth.

Dali's wife and great inspiration, Gala, appears in the deck as the Empress. Her interest in mysticism possibly introduced

Dali to the Tarot. (According to some accounts the deck began as a commission for the James Bond film, *Live and Let Die*. When that connection fell through, Dali went on to create his Tarot with the help of Amanda Lear. The film-makers then commissioned a less renowned artist, Fergus Hall, whose Tarot of the Witches can be found in the section on Popular Tarots.)

In most of the cards Dali remains close to traditional designs, though often expanding or playing with them. In the Chariot we see a dark figure with three flames: by the head, for intellect, the heart, for emotion, and the groin, for sexuality. On the front of the chariot the forms and paint suggest a mask.

In contrast to this complexity Temperance shows a cartoon-like angel, a nymphet mixing a cocktail. We can guess that the virtue of temperance did not appeal to a man as excessive as Dali.

A few cards depart radically from previous versions. The Devil resembles more the modern image of the Fool, a figure leaping off a cliff. Dark arms push the hermaphroditic figure. They suggest desires pushing us to destruction. On the card of the World we find three women, taken from *The Judgement of Paris* by Lucas Cranach the Elder. They wear chains, like the slaves in traditional versions of the Devil. Behind them we see a face similar to the mask on the Chariot. More than any other, this dreamlike card, frightening and mysterious, evokes the primal quality that made surrealism such a major force in the twentieth century, and Salvador Dali its most famous practitioner.

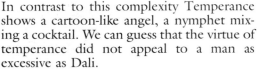

I Tarocchi di Andrea Picini

The Tarot of Andrea Picini mingles complex and precise designs with occult ideas, sexuality both implied and explicit, and political satire. The paintings place soft, often shadowy people, usually nude, within geometric forms. We see this in the Fool and the World (curiously the Fool resembles a cricket player). There are often words, as in the Moon, or the Ace of Cups, but these function more as images than explanations.

The political nature of the cards may belong more to Ugo Moretti's book about them than the pictures themselves. For the Pope, Moretti writes, 'The Pope no longer has the Keys of Wisdom, but has substituted them with the picklocks of Calculation.' He adds, 'This is the card of Politicians, Bankers, and in general those who love money.' The picture shows a figure kneeling down before an ornate couch, perhaps an implied comment on psychoanalysis.

Even without Moretti's explanations the complex designs would suggest an esoteric, yet personal, even obscure, interpretation. According to the commentary, Picini has changed various signs and elements due to 'calculations' and changes in the constellations. Since the positions of the stars in relation to the Earth certainly change over time the point is potentially an important one. The cards themselves, however, do not give this information in any clear way. Moretti claims that Picini has adapted the Tarot to modern experiences, creating a 'more easily assimilated iconography'. Provocative, yes; easily assimilated, not very likely.

The nudes, usually shown in silhouette and without faces, are mostly female. Moretti describes them as androgynous, merging the sexes. The Empress's womb is an abstract image with a very slight suggestion of male genitals. At her feet crouch four men, one

with a dark face. He is 'the "difficult" one, the homosexual, the degenerate, the albino'. Moretti (and presumably Picini, if we can take Moretti as a reliable witness to the artist's intentions) sees these qualities as exotic. He goes on to describe the Empress as the card of 'Prostitutes, Adulterers, Lesbians. . .'

The suits are called 'Seeds', an idea not really developed. Moretti compares them to what he calls the 'four sexes', a term he does not explain, though at one point the text refers to male, female, homosexual, and transexual.

The Seed cards show the same complexity and precision as the Trumps. The pictures include the name and number complementing the forms, as in the Four of Wands, or the Three of Coins. The emphasis remains on eroticism joined to abstraction, as in the Knight of Cups where horses rear up beside a

nude, while behind them, more vivid than the figures, shine concentric circles.

The cards themselves come with a booklet, but there is also a separate book with reproductions of the pictures. The colour tones in the book are often quite different from those

on the cards. The borders are red on the cards, black in the book, and many (though not all) the cards appear in the book darker and more intense.

Three Historically Based Tarots

When Vito Arienti began his Edizioni del Solleone he reprinted rare and historical Tarots. For his first modern deck he commissioned a radically re-imagined Tarot from the artist Elisabetta Cassari (see Story-telling Tarots). Since then, while continuing to publish Cassari he also has published a number of new decks based on historical themes. The three shown here include two by Amerigo Folchi. The Tarocco Storico del Palio Di Pistoia rearranges the trump and court cards to tell a history based on the twelfth-century Festival of Pistoia. The other, Omaggio a Erté, merges Folchi's own style with inspiration gained from the great Art Deco illustrator, Erté. The third deck, by Maria Teresa Perosino and Sergio Panza, is also a homage, in this case to Valentina Visconti, who according to legend brought the Tarot from Italy to France in the fourteenth century.

I Tarocchi di Valentina Visconti

Valentina Visconti belonged to the family for whom the first known Tarot cards were painted. When she married, her dowry included the town of Asti. In 1389, on the way to meet her husband, she stopped in the town to enjoy the annual festival. According to the short text accompanying the cards the visit 'initiated a splendid period for Asti's art and economy'.

This bit of historical information becomes the springboard for Perosino and Panza's deck. The two artists spent years researching both the festival and the Visconti family. The costumes belong to the period of Valentina, the beginning of the Renaissance.

According to the booklet, many early Tarot decks were done *tarocatto*, in which a stylet engraves gold leaf. To imitate this technique the artists have developed an ornate drawing style. This style lacks the solidity and depth of the early cards. For one thing, the black and white drawings miss the glorious colour of some of the cards associated with the Visconti court. For another, as in a number of other contemporary decks, the figures have an overly sweet quality. We see this in the Fool, or Justice.

Despite the unrealistic prettiness, there are a number of imaginative details in the pictures. In Justice an eye appears in the desert rock. Death is a bowman with an instrument at his feet. In Strength a strongman (Hercules?) strangles a two-headed serpent, while behind we see the tents of the festival.

The Palio d' Asti continues to the present day, with people dressed in medieval costumes. It ends with a horse race. In honour of this race the deck adds ten cards to the usual seventy-eight. These consist of five prizes given to the winners, plus five attributes needed to win. The prizes are Palio (banner), Speroni (spurs), Monere (coins), Gallo (cock) and Acciuga (anchovies). The attributes are Conoscenza (knowledge), Coraggio (cour-

age), Intrigo (intrigue), Astuzia (astuteness) and Liberta (freedom).

The leaflet gives a method of using the cards to forecast the outcome of the annual race. We can guess that many people over the centuries have tried doing this with the Tarot, with other decks and for other races.

Tarocco Storico del Palio di Pistoia

Amerigo Folchi's Pistoia Tarot commemorates another festival, that of the founding of the town of Pistoia in northern Italy. Folchi too researched the historical background, studying in the library of Pistoia to make sure the costumes were right. A number of the cards depict the architecture of the town, such as the Sun and Temperance. The Star shows the town as a whole. The four Aces display heraldic devices related to the city's main gates. The chess-board patterns on the Aces follow through in the other pip cards.

The deck rearranges the trump and court cards to tell the history of Pistoia. It begins with the Emperor, commemorating the founding of the town as a free community. Various other cards show different stages or important events. The Devil shows, in allegorical form, the robbery of the treasury of San Iacopo in the church of San Zeno in 1293. The robbery involved political battles between the Blacks and the Whites. One of the conspirators, a leader of the Pistoise

19 - IL SOLE

17 - LA STELLA

Asso di denari

Asso di bastoni

4 - L'IMPERATORE

15 - IL DIAVOLO

quattro di spade

Blacks, was Vanni Fucci, who appears as a sufferer in hell in *The Divine Comedy* by Dante. Dante himself can be seen with his book in the upper right corner of the card.

The final seven trumps (also out of order) show social and allegorical figures, such as the Magician, who is described as a charlatan and is seen giving a Tarot reading in a form similar to the Celtic cross. We can guess that Folchi is commenting on the modern use and interpretation of the cards. Strength is drawn as St George killing a dragon while the sun blazes behind him. The last card is Death, painted in sumptuous robes with black clouds behind him and a sun setting or rising at his feet.

1 - IL MAGO

11 - LA FORZA

13 - LA MORTE

Omaggio a Erté

Folchi's second deck is simpler in content, but more elegant in design. Indeed, following Erté means that elegance becomes the primary focus for the entire deck. As with the Pistoia, the cards are beautifully printed, on quality cardboard, with colours that are both deeper and more subtle than those on most decks.

Because Erté was a fashion illustrator for *Harper's Bazaar* the figures are all female and dressed in costumes both magnificent and outrageous. The Devil shows a bare-breasted woman delicately suffering in the flames of Hell. Death is poised in a gauzy dress, her face half fashion-model, half skull. For the Lover we see a pair of innocent girls who may or may not be lesbians.

The stylized women appear throughout the Minor cards as well, including the male court cards.

The Tarots of Osvaldo Menegazzi

Like Vito Arienti, Osvaldo Menegazzi publishes small editions of historical Tarot decks from his private collection. At the same time he has, for some years, published a series of remarkable decks painted by himself, each one with a particular theme. The images are painted with great clarity against a plain background.

Ruota di Fortuna

Regina di bastoni

IL DIAVOLO

RE DI COPPE

The realism of the style gives a solidity to the images, which are carefully chosen for their aptness. In the Animal Tarot, the owl as the Devil draws on the European tradition of describing owls as evil. Often the decks seem trivial at first, but with an underlying intensity. In the Collection Tarot, the use of ritual masks for the Queens gives the whole deck a sense of mystery which deepens our reactions to the toys and statues shown on the other cards.

The clarity of the paintings can give them an almost hallucinatory quality, a counter to the seeming lightness of the themes. In the Divinatory Flowers, and even in the witty Fantastic Shoes, the more we look at the images the more we get a sense of something deeper. The Divinatory Flowers deck comes with a short text telling us that meditation on these pictures can 'free us from the forces that oppress us'. This is a very different enter-

IL BAGATTO

L' ANGELO

L' IMPERATORE

LA FORTUNA

prise from the intricate symbolism (and often rather weak art) of many esoteric Tarots. The goal is the same, but the method is different. Menegazzi seeks to touch something essential in the psyche with these images directly out of nature.

Some decks are clearly meant as comic, with others more serious. Menegazzi has painted both a Smokers' Tarot and a Tobacco Tarot. The first mimics the wood-cut style of old decks, but in a cartoon-like way. The contrast of the pipes with the classic Tarot scenes can be extremely funny. The Tobacco Tarot (which comes in a small metal tobacco case) is closer to Menegazzi's usual style, finding images that subtly match the particular theme.

By contrast to these two, the Musical Tarot is more elaborate, taking most of its images from grand opera. The Empress comes from Puccini's *Turandot*, the Sun from *Aida*, with the Ace of Coins as Verdi himself.

Two decks seek directly to evoke that inner awakening mentioned with the Flowers cards. In the Divinatory Hands Tarot disembodied hands hold symbolic objects against a sky dotted with clouds. A commentary by Alberto Tanturri describes the deck as 'a means of meditating on our reason for being'. In the Papess we see the hand holding the Bible, open at 'In the beginning was the word. . .'. The clasped hands on the Lovers convey intimacy in the simplest form. The woman's hand extends down from heaven,

while the man's reaches up to clasp hold of it. There is a quality of humanity reaching for the divine. In the World, the callipers measuring the ball hint at Freemasonry.

Menegazzi painted the Sardinia Tarot as an homage to the people, and the magic, of

Sardinia. The trump figures belong to an ancient tradition. This history gives the bronze statues a concentrated power.

Strands of coral surround the statues.

According to a short text with the cards the Sardinians use coral for magic and healing. It brings messages from the Gods of the sea to the 'power of the Earth'.

The Haindl Tarot

Of all the decks described in this book I know the Haindl Tarot best, for I have not only written a book describing these cards, I have also spent many hours discussing them with Hermann and Erica Haindl. Hermann Haindl has worked many years creating intense dreamlike paintings expressing the agony of modern humanity against a back-ground of spirituality. He considers his Tarot his life's testament. He has put into it his own experiences: as a teenager in the time of the Nazis, as a prisoner of war in Russia, as someone whose own life awakened through art, as a campaigner to save the environment, as a spiritual traveller in India and Native America. When he decided to use Egypt as

the source for the Swords court cards, he first studied the mythology and beliefs, then journeyed to Egypt itself, so that he could paint the four cards from within the culture and the land.

The pictures on the Haindl Tarot are vivid and compelling, with virtually every card reimagined.

The Chariot rushes forward through a foaming sea, chased by a roaring beast. It evokes a shamanic journey through terror and ecstasy. The Hanged Man brings a joyous vision of surrender. Odin, who as the young Emperor, turns his back on the World Tree, here returns to the Earth. The shape of the land implies a pregnant woman lying on her back, recalling the ancient belief in the Earth as a Goddess, a spiritual being unified and alive. In the Star we see her personified as Gaea, the ancient Mother. She bends down to wash her hair, and in that naturalistic gesture we see the essential belief of the Haindl Tarot – that the Earth will wash herself clean of hate and fear as well as destruction, that, faced with the choice of universal death or a return to sacred respect, we will manage to choose life.

The Haindl Tarot reworks mythology to its own ends. The story that inspired Haindl's Hanged Man is Odin's self-sacrifice to achieve the Runes from the Well at the base of the World Tree. As a patriarchal God Odin did not offer himself to the Earth, but simply 'myself to myself'. He also gave up an eye to Mimir. Symbolically this indicates the difficulty of turning inwards, to the unconscious. But in the Hanged Man surrender allows reversal without violence. In the Father of Cups we see a more historical version of the myth, and there the card is more problematic, signifying arrogance as well as power.

The deck seeks to blend the spiritual traditions of different lands. The Fool wears the costume of a European jester, but the colours on his sleeve are the sacred colours of the Lakota nation of North America. In the Hierophant the theme of tradition comes out as three generations of Jews studying the sacred books. The card is set in the attic room (used for meditation) of Haindl's studio.

Haindl made the tradition card Jewish partly as symbol of reconciliation between Germans and Jews. This was also one of the motives for using Runes as well as Hebrew letters on each of the trumps. Like the Hebrew alphabet the Runes are both ordinary letters and an esoteric system. They form part

of the native tradition of north-west Europe. When Haindl matched them with the Hebrew letters (using the Runic system of German author Zoltan Szabo) he found some strong correspondences. On the Empress, both the letter and the Rune mean 'Door'.

There is actually another Rune found within the Empress card. The lines within the crystal above her form the Rune Hagall, or 'Hailstone' (following the order of the Runic alphabet Hagall appears on the

Chariot). In the ancient system this Rune contained the primal pattern for the universe. Along with the hexagram enclosing it we can form all the Runes from the lines contained within Hagall. This gives it the title 'Mother of Runes', fitting for the Empress, who is the Triple Goddess. It appears in many places throughout the deck, in the Minor as well as the Major cards. We see it in the Three of Wands and the Six of Stones.

For the Minor cards (two-ten) Haindl began with the title and the basic theme of the card. He derived these primarily from the Thoth Tarot of Aleister Crowley. Then he looked through his own previous work for a painting, or more often a fragment from a painting, which expressed that essential idea. The emblems for the suit were then painted on to the previous work. In the best of these

cards the two elements work together to produce a unified picture. In the Six of Stones the hole in the rock completes the shape of the Rune. The hole in the Nine of Cups allows the water of life to break through the stone wall. The winter stillness on the Two of Swords joins with the balanced swords to produce the theme of a truce.

Each of the pip cards is matched to an *I*

Ching hexagram. Because there are only thirty-six cards, but sixty-four hexagrams, Haindl chose these subjectively. Usually he chose hexagrams with the same idea as the card, but in some cases, where the Tarot goes very far in a certain direction the *I Ching* balances it. The Six of Wands signifies 'Victory', a concept which Haindl found troubling for it implied war and the idea of losers. Therefore he added hexagram Two, the 'Receptive', the primal hexagram of gentleness and the Earth.

The Aces connect the Minor cards to the court cards, seen here (and in some other decks) as a separate group. For the court cards the Haindl Tarot enters the mythology of different lands. Each suit represents a direction as well as an element. They are Wands-Fire-East-India (Asia), Cups-Water-North-Europe, Swords-Air-South-Egypt (Africa), Stones-Earth-West-America. The Aces join with the court cards. They show primal images from each of the religious cultures. The Ace of Wands shows a lingam and yoni (a phallic stone and a lotus with water to

symbolize the vulva), the Ace of Cups is the Holy Grail (this was the reason for choosing Cups for North).

Instead of the medieval King, Queen, Knight, Page, the Haindl Tarot uses Mother, Father, Daughter, Son. The Mothers are all archaic figures from mythology, such as Spider Woman for Stones, or the thirty thousand-year-old Goddess statue found near Willendorf for the Mother of Cups.

The Fathers signify the bringing of this archaic force into consciousness. Thus Odin brings up the Runes from the dark well at the base of the tree. The Fathers are Creator figures, such as Ra for Father of Swords. At the same time the Mothers come first, for true creative power originates in the Goddess. The Daughters and Sons show us the more personal sides of the mythologies, such as White Buffalo Woman for the Daughter of

Stones, or Krishna, India's most beloved figure, for the Son of Wands.

One card shows an historical person. The Son of Stones is a portrait of Chief Seattle, leader of the nation which once lived on the north-west coast of what is now the United States. When the Whites first came Seattle attempted to welcome them. Later, seeing his people on the edge of extinction, and the destruction of the land, he made a speech

before the United States Congress. He spoke of the rights of the native people, but also of the animals and the Earth itself. In his Tarot Hermann Haindl has joined his own voice to the Son of Stones.

The Tarot Garden of Niki de St Phalle

For the student or collector of Tarot there has never been anything like it. Even before your car arrives at the property you can see it in the distance. Flashes of bright colour above the treetops, the Tuscan sun bouncing off ceramic and glass. When you come up the driveway, and the gate slides away, the statues rise up from the hillside like a shamanic world of dreams. Before you stands the black metal Wheel of Fortune, and beyond that the white steps leading up to the mouth of the High Priestess. You can enter through the mouth itself and come out behind the Empress, or else turn right, walk under the archway of the Sun God, past the cartoon face of the Pope, past the Lovers and the Tree of Life, and between the feet of Justice.

High Priestess and Magician

Sun God and Pope

Top left   *Pope, Lovers and Tree*

Left   *Two views of the Tower*

Above   *Justice*

De St Phalle has combined the Magician and the High Priestess into one statue, a recognition of the necessary unity of these two basic principles. The Magician is on top, a seeming reversal since the Magician comes first in the Major Arcana. But if the Magician signifies light and action, and the High Priestess stillness and darkness, then the High Priestess belongs below, as an underpinning to the Magician's mirrored brightness. The serpent of knowledge, of Gnosis, curls up to the High Priestess. Both their mouths are open, in conversation. According to an article in *Architectural Digest* the mirrors on the Magician came almost by accident. De St Phalle had made the hand above the head, only to find it too large, unbalancing the statue. It occurred to her that covering it with small mirrors would render it less imposing. The effect worked so well she went on to cover the head as well, and then used the same technique for the Tower.

The Tower too changed from its original design. At first, it belonged to the Emperor's castle. When she finished it, de St Phalle panicked. It was too large; it overpowered the castle and everything around it. She called Jean Tinguely, her husband and long-time collaborator (the Wheel of Fortune fountain is by Tinguely). He added the open top and the wheels of machinery. With the mirrors it became the Tower, flashing in the sun behind the other statues.

Some people seeing the statues, or photos of them, have remarked on their resemblance

to the fantastic architecture of Gaudí, in Barcelona. In fact, Niki de St Phalle was very impressed by Gaudí from the moment she saw his work. Years ago, she promised herself she would one day create a mythological garden of monumental statues. And then she discovered the Tarot, and realized that the ancient images would give the garden a much sharper focus.

If Gaudí inspired the work it remains very much the creation of Niki de St Phalle. The childlike playfulness, the intense colours of the ceramics (as shown in Adam and Eve from the Lovers), these are her trademarks. Though many of the 'cards' are several stories high, they are primarily statues, not buildings, as in the work of Gaudí. This gives them a greater freedom of form. The Pope consists of three lines for the head, plus eyes (three of them), nose and mouth. Some statues do have rooms, and the Empress is an actual house, the artist's home during the several years of the project.

The Empress-Sphinx was unfinished when I visited the garden. The building was complete, but the ceramics were only half done. The picture gives us a sense of the method of working. The actual statue is reinforced concrete poured into a mould. De St Phalle then marks in diagrams the colours and shapes of the tiles. These are made by a specialist in a separate workshop. Each tile receives a long series of firings in the kiln to protect it from the weather. When the tiles arrive the artist and her crew work together, placing them one at a time.

Many of the statues, including the Empress and the High Priestess-Magician, are made for people to climb up or go inside. The photo of Temperance is taken from the stairway along the side of the High Priestess. The dark blue angel, with her golden wings, dances atop a kind of igloo. Inside is a chapel to the Black Madonna. Inside the mouth of the Magician is another chapel, filled with mythological and esoteric images. The photo of Strength (unfinished, without tiles) comes from inside the mouth of the High Priestess.

The female Temperance brings out a vital theme in the work, that of women's experi-

Left *Lovers*

ence. The statues have a feminine fullness of form, a lushness and sensuality. At the time of my visit, de St Phalle was finding herself blocked from finishing the Hermit. When I told her of the various women's decks, and the way some of them replaced the Hermit with the Crone she realized that she had not been able to visualize the statue because she had not recognized consciously that it needed a woman's face.

When I visited Niki de St Phalle she asked me to do a reading using the statues as cards. Since we could not shuffle the statues I asked the artist to draw a diagram of their placement on the property. We then read these as a layout. Next, her son-in-law, writer and photographer Laurent Fabius, took Polaroid photos of each of the statues. With these as cards, the artist shuffled them, and we laid them in the new order on top of the different places in the diagram. This not only gave us a new spread, it also allowed us to compare the two, seeing how one card had 'transmuted'

Above *Empress*
Above right *Temperance*
Right *Strength*

into another. Finally, we went outside (we had been sitting inside the Empress) and walked from statue to statue, seeing the actual relationships they formed on the land itself. The system worked so well that Niki de St Phalle hopes eventually to publish an aerial photograph of the entire garden, plus a set of photos to use as cards.

CHAPTER 2
Popular Tarots

As a card game, or a device for fortune-telling, the Tarot has always sought a wide audience. The term 'popular' could belong to any deck which does not appear in a limited art edition and does not shower us with secret glyphs or obscure references. Nevertheless, we can say that certain decks take a very direct approach to the Tarot images. They avoid complex doctrines, they do not link the cards to external ideas, such as fantasy stories or cultural traditions, they do not present themselves as fine art for a specialist public. In short, they aim themselves at the average person who has an interest in Tarot.

This does not make such decks inferior. On the contrary, they often show a highly individual style as well as a great deal of artistic freshness. This comes from the freedom from specific doctrines and official images. The Simplified Tarot plays with the trump figures and court cards in often hilarious ways. Tarot Maddonni presents a unique vision, surreal, comic, presenting its ideas through form and style rather than complex symbols. Both the Tarot of the Witches and the Prediction Tarot seek a dreamlike effect. Both use pared-down figures in limited backgrounds. Beyond that, however, they take opposite approaches, the Tarot of the Witches with distorted cartoon-like figures, the Prediction Tarot with realistic people set among clouds and on mountain-tops.

Most popular decks, such as the Simplified Tarot and the Prediction Tarot emphasize fortune-telling. They describe themselves as easy to understand, with simple meanings for the beginning diviner. Sometimes the actual pictures will suggest far more than we would guess from the descriptions in their instruction booklets.

Decks for a wide audience sometimes align themselves with current trends. The Hanson-Roberts Tarot reworks the famous Rider pack, but it manages to slip in some small references to Neo-Paganism, particularly in the Hierophant. It also reduces the Rider pack's symbolic structure and gives the images a modern dynamism. If a deck takes too much from fashions of the day it runs the risk of becoming dated in ten or fifteen years. The New Tarot, from the early 1970s, was one of the first decks to re-imagine thoroughly the traditional pictures. It anticipates a number of trends that later came into full bloom. Some of the scenes, however, and many of the descriptions, reveal the fashionable preoccupations of that time. We find the same limitation in the wildly imaginative Neuzeit Tarot of Walter Wegmuller. The style resembles psychedelic posters from the 1960s, with many of the figures dressed like members of hippie communes. The New Tarot has the 'excuse' of belonging to its period. Wegmuller's deck appeared in 1982.

The New Tarot

Published in 1973, The New Tarot actually belongs to an earlier period than most of the decks shown in this book. It came towards the end of the Tarot popularity boom generated by the hippie movement. At the same time it pointed the way to the later 'Tarot Renaissance' (a term from Gary Ross of *Tarot Network News*) for it forms one of the first fully re-imagined Tarots, with all the pictures recast, some of them quite dramatically.

The technique appears to be woodcuts, which links the deck with some of the Tarots from hundreds of years ago. Both the Tower and the Moon work through carefully drafted designs. The Tower remains closer to traditional images, adding the circle of dancing lightning and the sea. The Moon uses the standard pictorial elements of two dogs, two towers, and a road, but completely recasts them by making the lunar Goddess herself the road. The description says, 'The Spirit joins head, heart and body', a radical interpretation of the Moon experience. Judgement goes much further from tradition. Instead of a Christian ressurection it depicts a Pagan rejoicing. Notice how the road and the circle form the female symbol. 'The Lady returned' says the text, which also shows the 1960s influence with the line 'All the tribes dance the Rites of Spring.'

Before the New Tarot, designers of new decks tended to see two options for the Minor Arcana. They could adapt the Rider pack scenes from Pamela Smith, or else return to the pattern designs for the pip cards. Jack Hurley, Rae Hurley, and John Horler chose instead to develop their own scenes.

The text for the Nine of Swords demonstrates a very dated quality in some of the descriptions: 'Big Momma invites you to cut up the pig at her revolutionary thanksgiving party.' The Queen of Fire is described as 'black, beautiful . . . bossy broad'. We read of 'energy rip-offs' and 'communes' and 'C'mon, baby, light my fire [pyre?].' And yet the picture for the Queen of Fire gives us a whole new image, opening possibilities beyond the description.

The Princess of Swords points the way to some of the later mythological and Goddess-oriented Tarots, for it describes her as Kore, daughter of Demeter, and Persephone, wife of Hades. In general, however, this aspect is not developed in the other court cards, which emphasize astrological connections. The Knights are described as messengers, setting them apart from the other court cards to leave twelve, the number of signs in the zodiac. The Golden Dawn took a similar approach, except that it set the Princesses aside, describing them as the basic elements. The New Tarot chooses the Knights for the sensible reason that playing cards evolved with only the Jack (Page), Queen, and King. The Knight, therefore, is the extra card that became lost, and now returns with its message.

A number of cards, especially in the Minor Arcana, play with images and ideas. The Three of Circles shows a group of people earnestly discussing a rigid structure while ignoring the circles of harmony above them. The Five of Cups depicts a comic 'wild party or brawl'. The Nine of Circles gives us a lady of the manor arguing with her gardener. When we look closer we see the gardener's goat-legs. The text says, 'Pan versus the female chauvinist sow', another dated expression.

A number of cards show naked women or other female images. They tend to be more realistic than many decks, less Hollywood beautiful and more the actual shape of women's bodies. We see this in the Two of Swords, which celebrates 'Relations between women and generations'. The change of the

swords to sickles looks towards the later women's decks, for sickles symbolize both the Moon and agriculture, two aspects of the Great Mother. The soft and pretty Six of Wands, the kind of image one sees in so many popular Tarots, is described satirically as 'an upfront male chauvinist sex fantasy'.

The Simplified Tarot

This small black and white deck (many of the popular Tarots are the same size as ordinary playing cards, or even smaller) describes itself as 'the easiest fortune-telling Tarot ever'. The Belgian edition goes even further, describing the deck as 'the poor person's Tarot'. When we see Jan Bauwens's highly original witty pictures, we can suspect the description as at least partly tongue-in-cheek. The pictures often undercut the 'simplified' descriptions.

THE HIEROPHANT

THE LOVERS

THE CHARIOT

The surrealist Hierophant, with his large hands and billowing skirts, is described as 'the highest spiritual authority on Earth. And what he approves God will approve', a statement we can hardly take seriously. The description for the Lovers says (simplified) 'In Medieval days love had to be above all very chaste, otherwise sin ensued.' The fortune-telling advice says 'Honorable conduct will bring about a joyous romance.' The hilarious picture gives a far greater dimension to the words. The Chariot (like the Hierophant) demonstrates a certain suspicion of the grand images and pronouncements found in less simple Tarots. We see a pompously dressed figure in a simple cart drawn by a horse wearing a grand plume. The description begins with a comment on traditional versions: 'This was for everyone a triumphal carriage' and then adds, 'but apparently there is always the deep awareness that few triumphs last.'

THE POPESS

THE EMPRESS

THE EMPEROR

The cards express comical ideas in a few lines. The distorted, shortened figures satirize traditional images. The Papess appears sly, a comment on the Church, the Empress frowns at her absent subjects, while the Emperor's giant moustache and the way his beard merges into his armour and his throne create a pompous ruler whose glare is undercut by his foolishness.

Some of the cards show a playful fantasy. The Hermit appears on a magical bridge.

The Wheel has a figure turning a crank to make the simplified zodiac wheel (only six signs) go round. The picture suggests in a direct way that we bring about our own luck. Or is the figure a petulant child, a comment on the idea of the Fates? The Tower gives us a marvellous image of the tower as a person, while the Star presents a fantasy far removed from traditional pictures.

The suit cards, unfortunately, show only the emblems. It would have been interesting

THE HERMIT

THE WHEEL

THE TOWER

THE STAR

FIVE OF DISKS

THREE OF SWORDS

KING OF DISKS

QUEEN OF CUPS

KNIGHT OF SWORDS

KNAVE OF WANDS

to see what the artist might have done with the more open possibilities of the suits. Though the Cups and Wands are standard, the Swords appear more like knives, while the disks all display an open hand.

The court cards are done with style, though with less imagination than the trumps. The Knights satirize the macho warrior. We see them laden down with armour – and muscles. They overpower their small horses, so that their feet rest on the ground, making battle, even movement, impossible. The Knaves, by contrast, all stand in this stylish way, concerned perhaps with their clothes. The Kings display the pomposity found in many of the trumps, while the Queens seem more balanced, but at the same time less developed as ideas.

The Simplified Tarot belies its name with a highly individual play of satire and fantasy.

Tarot Maddonni

The style of this deck resembles that of the Simplified Tarot. Again we find a distortion of forms, as in the Hermit and the High Priestess. We also find a penchant for comedy, as in the Pope.

The art in the Tarot Maddonni, however,

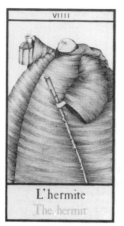

L'hermite
The hermit

La Papesse
The High Priestess

Le Pape
The Pope

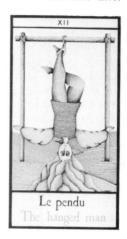

Le pendu
The hanged man

Le Soleil
The Sun

on an abstraction of hills, or the calm, radiant Sun-face shining down on tiny stick-figures. The backgrounds for all these cards are plain white; the landscapes are reduced to waving lines for the sea, simple curves for hills, or flat surfaces.

The booklet for this French deck describes the cards as having 'precise' esoteric designs. In fact, if we take the Tarot de Marseilles as the basic Tarot, and such decks as Aleister Crowley's Thoth Tarot as an esoteric example, we will see that the Tarot Maddonni lacks symbolic structures or abstract forms, or precise symbols. The cards affect us by their unique style, and their free imagination. In a way, they suggest an alternative to esoteric Tarots. Rather than follow a fixed set of ideas or correspondences, they stimulate us aesthetically.

is more complex, with a wonderful use of colour and flowing forms. Notice the billowing robes of the High Priestess, the way the hair of the Hanged Man falls in thick tresses

L'Etoile
The Star

La Force
Force

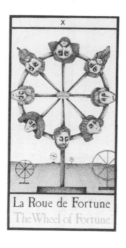

La Roue de Fortune
The Wheel of Fortune

The Star shows us the expected woman with a jug, though only one in contrast to the usual two, with their symbolic references to polarity, conscious and unconscious and so on. Sylvia Maddonni has simplified the picture, yet made it much more expressive. The water irrigates a desert, while the woman herself is wild, uncivilized. Stars cling to the ends of her matted hair. In Force we perhaps could describe as 'esoteric' the way in which the woman's hair mirrors the fiery mane of the lion, or the way the lion's head is distorted into flames. But this would be an intuitive esoterica, rather than a conceptual one.

In the Wheel of Fortune, too, we get suggestions of inner meanings, particularly in the empty wheels reaching into the distance. We could also find varied meanings in the heads mounted on the wheel. These meanings would be subjective, in comparison with the developed ideas of most Wheel of Fortune cards. Notice the lack of mythological images. We see no Egyptian or biblical beasts, no alchemical glyphs, no Hebrew writing on the spokes. Instead, the picture uses simple human forms to create a sense of mystery.

Only the Devil displays a fantasy figure. Notice again the lack of symbolism, and the fact that the figures on leashes are humans

Le Diable
The Devil

L'amoureux
The lover

Le Mat
The Fool

Le Bateleur
The Magician

rather than demons. The Devil stays close to tradition; the Lovers moves further away, keeping Cupid, but showing a group of couples, some of whom appear in love, and others bored.

Most of the cards emphasize style over complex imagery. Fantasy emerges again in the Fool, with his lines of string holding various symbolic objects, including a card representing himself. A cage contains an abstract peacock, which then reappears in the Magician, as if from under his hat. We can develop symbolic interpretations from these cards, just as we can from the fact that the Tower card lies on top of the pack on the Magician's table. These interpretations are likely to be subjective, more like stories.

Satire does not appear as strong an

element here as in some other individualized decks; we do find it in such cards as The

Le Chariot
The Chariot

Roy de Baton
The King of Clubs

Roy de Coupe
The King of Cups

Reyne de Coupe
The Queen of Cups

Cavalier de Coupe
The Knight of Cups

Valet de Coupe
The Knave of Cups

Pope (so often a target in decks from Catholic countries), and perhaps the foppish Charioteer. Satire comes through more strongly in the court cards, particularly the Kings. The King of Clubs seems hardly able to hold up his staff. He might suggest Don Quixote. A romantic, he wears a brooch with a woman's face.

The Cups family emphasizes the comical side of the deck. Their giant curls, the Queen's suspicious look, the Knave's sneakiness, and especially the childlike Knight on his hobbyhorse, make us wish for a series of stories about their absurd behaviour.

Roy d'Epée
The King of Swords

Reyne d'Epée
The Queen of Swords

Cavalier de Deniers
The Knight of Money

Reyne de Deniers
The Queen of Money

The Swords figures too appear humorous, with the King and Queen staring into the sky, as if lost in the clouds. Swords usually symbolize the element Air; in most decks this leads to images either of wisdom or sorrow. Interestingly, the Coins cards are shown more seriously, with gentleness in the Queen and Knight.

As in the Simplified Tarot, the artist has chosen to do very little with the Minor cards, simply displaying the emblem of the suit. The Sword hilt suggests the traditional Magician's hat, while the Coin bears an arrow pointing upwards, allowing symbolic interpretation.

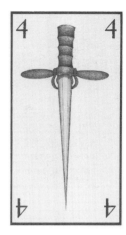

Rolla Nordic Tarot

The Nordic Tarot bases itself partly on traditional European designs, as in the Juggler and the Lovers, and partly on the more modern esoteric images, as in the Priestess, the Chariot, and the Sun.

The Priestess holds a partly rolled-up Torah, as in the Rider pack. The Chariot, however, has the older image of horses, rather than sphinxes. They are also both the same, rather than one black and one white to symbolize polarity. The card of the Sun follows the Rider pack quite closely, with a single child on a horse carrying a banner instead of two children in a garden holding hands. However,

the horse stands in a circle within the garden, which does suggest more traditional versions.

The deck comes in black and white, with instructions for colouring. A number of esoteric decks have taken this approach, notably Paul Foster Case's Builders of the Adytum deck, and the deck of the Church of Light. In both these examples, the student joins a study group and receives precise instructions for colouring each card. In this way, the deck becomes personal while at the same time following the occult tradition, in which each colour carries a special meaning.

The Nordic Tarot gives colouring direc-

THE JUGGLER

THE LOVERS

THE PRIESTESS

THE CHARIOT

tions – but it also tells you to make your own choices. On the one hand, the booklet says, 'The colour suggestions correspond to the symbolism of the cards', but it also says, 'There is no one right way to colour any card except the one you like best.' This last idea represents a radical departure from previous occult belief. It also marks a feature of many new decks. Very often, if a designer expects that people will colour in black and white cards, she or he gives no directions at all. Outside the strictly esoteric Tarots, personal expression has replaced fixed correspondences.

The style of these cards is very simplistic

THE SUN

THE WORLD

THE BLACK MAGICIAN

MAGUS

THE ENCHANTRESS

KING OF SWORDS

HORSEMAN OF WANDS

PAGE OF PENTACLES

(not 'simplified', which can be a subtle technique). Though they have a certain charm they do not contribute much in the way of new ideas or images. The themes are undeveloped, such as in the World, or the Black Magician (Devil), which makes it hard to take them seriously.

The Black Magician is one of three cards with new names. None of them, however, do much to change the pictures. The Magus (the Fool) derives directly from the Oswald Wirth Tarot (late nineteenth century).

The court cards resemble the figures on playing cards, ornate, but without clear meaning. The double quality of the King of Swords and some other cards may contain a particular idea, though this is not clear. The Knights are named 'Horseman'.

The booklet, written by Rolla Nordic, takes a very naive approach to the Tarot, accepting legends about its origin that few people today take very seriously. Nordic mentions, with astonishment, seeing gamblers in Algiers 'actually using the Tarot for card games', whereas any historical account of the cards will always emphasize their use as a game long before the first esoteric descriptions appeared (at least publicly).

The Prager Tarot

At first glance this deck resembles the Nordic Tarot. Such figures as the Magician, Strength, and the Star, appear almost the same.

However, this is because both decks use traditional woodcut designs as their inspiration. The commentary, by Stuart Kaplan, refers to the tradition in Prague, Czechoslovakia, of artistic cardmakers, especially W. Sewera, who published cards in the nineteenth century. In fact, the Prager Tarot has almost nothing to do with Sewera's elegant and imaginative Animal Tarock (illustrated in Vol. I of Kaplan's *Encylopedia of Tarot*). The commentary also reminds us of Prague's very important occult tradition, with the famous Golem legend as an example. This too hardly seems to influence the actual cards.

Some of the designs show an individual flair (the artist's name is not given). The Papess appears veiled, with a black cloth, suggestive of bat-wings, behind her head. The Empress may have a shaved head. We see a lunar crescent at her feet, with seven stars, for the Pleiades, above her head. A 'Fire' triangle, upward-pointing, usually a symbol of maleness, appears over the genital area. The booklet refers to this as a triangle of motherhood. The Charioteer, by contrast, has flowing blonde hair bedecked with flowers, and a somewhat feminine face.

The Minor cards, while not showing scenes, have occasional animals and objects to give them more life. The Ace of Wands bears a pair of salamanders, legendary animals associated in alchemy with the element of Fire. Noah's ark floats under the Ace of Cups, a serpent winds around the Ace of Swords, while on the Two of Coins a black bird, presumably a raven (associated mythologically

with death and the Underworld) holds one coin in its beak and another in its claws.

The court cards seem standard, if somewhat ornate. Variations come on the masked Servant of Swords and the Knight of Cups with a fish on his helmet. The Coins cards depict bird emblems, an indication of a link with the element of Air. This makes the Swords Earth, as demonstrated in plants on the suit cards and bulls, for Taurus (an Earth sign) on the King and Queen.

As usual in Tarock decks, the Prager Tarot contains fifty-four cards: twenty-two trumps,

sixteen court cards, and sixteen suit cards. Traditionally, Swords and Batons include ten through seven, but here they have Ace through Four, the same as Cups and Coins.

The most interesting contribution in this deck comes in the booklet rather than the cards themselves. There we learn first of all about geomancy practised by desert nomads who created 'a sort of runic system' of sixteen symbols, supposedly related to four elements, twelve zodiac signs, and the seven planets of ancient astrology. The booklet proposes this as the source of the sixteen suit

cards and sixteen court cards.

It then goes on to describe Chaldean astrology, which depended on twenty-one 'stations' of the Moon, and a group of specific stars and constellations ignored by modern astrology. Again, sadly, we find very little sign of this in the deck itself.

The card of the World links the usual Biblical beasts to four stars which 'form a roughly-shaped rectangle in the sky that frames the world'. The booklet claims that the letters in the upper right corner of each trump refer to these astrological links. In fact, they are simply Latin equivalents of the Hebrew letters found on Kabbalist Tarots. For instance, D on the Emperor comes from Daleth, and UV on the Lovers from Vav.

The Chaldean/geomantic suggestions open the possibility of a fascinating Tarot, with fresh images and mythological associations. Sadly, the Prager Tarot does very little with the ideas raised in the commentary.

The Neuzeit Tarot

The Neuzeit, or New Age, Tarot was created in 1982 by Walter Wegmuller, the same artist who did the earlier Zigeuner Tarot (see the section on Cultural Tarots). We find in both decks intense images and bizarre distorted figures among a riot of symbols. In both, the ideas mix esoteric systems with environmental concerns and hippie senti- mentality. In the Tower and Judgement we see images of technological civilization collapsing, with, in Judgement, nude figures rushing towards each other from holes in the Earth. The Hierophant sits with a group of admirers, as if in a commune, while the people in Strength and the Lover wear clothes that set them in the 1960s. A science fiction ele-

DIE ZERSTÖRUNG / THE TOWER / LA MAISON DIEU

DAS GERICHT / JUDGMENT / LE JUGEMENT

DIE KRAFT / STRENGTH / LA FORCE

DIE ENTSCHEIDUNG / THE LOVER / L'AMOUREUX

ment comes in with the comical robots on the World.

The cards are glutted with symbols, making them almost more chaotic than meaningful. Choosing at random, we find examples in the Queen, Knight, and Nine of Wands, cards so packed with images we would hardly know where to begin in any attempt to 'explain' them. They are hallucinatory rather than occult, reminding us of the melting forms in LSD art of the 1960s. Wegmuller is the sort of artist whom some might label a genius, and whom others would avoid at all cost.

In some   places, especially the Coins, Wegmuller becomes more comprehensible, with a sharp satirical edge. The Page of coins

runs a betting office, the Seven gives us contemporary polarities including 'micro' and 'macro business', while the Ace confronts us with starvation.

A number of the trumps are comical. In most versions of the Empress she holds an eagle shield. Here a live eagle hatches an eaglet. When we look closely at the Hermit,

we discover that the tree on lower left displays hands making obscene gestures. Wegmuller's Romany background does not figure so strongly in this deck as in the Zigeuner. We do find evidence of it on such cards as the Moon, where one tower represents contemporary urban civilization, while the other shows a medieval town with a Rom

caravan. The Knight of Cups is a Rom chieftain, a contrast to the King of Cups, who rules over a battle between police and radical demonstrators.

The descriptions, especially in the Minor cards, attempt to bring in ancient and tribal ideas. The booklet describes the wand as 'the guiding light of the nomadic tribes', and adds that one who can interpret them is likely to be a 'medicine man, a herbalist'. Since these professions have become quite scarce in the modern world the information is not likely to help very many people. Realistic application does not seem a major concern here.

Like the pictures, some descriptions mix esoterica with popular radicalism. The booklet tells us that the High Priestess 'defies the patriarchy and is absolute leader of all women'. It addes, 'With her scepter she conquers the fiery force of malehood whose semen she fertilizes'!

Some of the divinatory meanings given are absurdly specific. The King of Wands includes the information, 'Luck connected with air or space travel'. For the Emperor reversed, the first meaning is 'Impotence'. The meanings also include 'Mother complexes. Sexual neroses'. The High Priestess advises, 'Listen to the advice of your mother or a female fortune-teller'. Women Tarot readers (and mothers) may decide to use the Neuzeit Tarot just for that card alone.

Tarot of the Witches

The *Encyclopedia of Tarot* informs us that the Tarot of the Witches appeared in the James Bond film, *Live and Let Die*. The box and booklet for the cards leaves out this information, as if the publishers feared prospective buyers might distrust the deck. Serious followers of Wicca (the name used by modern Witches) still might feel their religion trivialized by the description on the box: 'Ideal for Tarot readings in covens and private meetings by Witches, Warlocks and followers of the occult'. The booklet, by Stuart Kaplan, attempts to give a fair description of modern witchcraft. It describes the structure of covens, and links the four directions of the 'magick circle' to the four suits of the Minor

Arcana. It also, however, includes such statements as 'the black witch tends to lean more towards mischievous and evil interpretations'.

The card designs are simple and dramatic, depending more on wit than symbolism. The painter, Fergus Hall, has sought a surreal, dreamlike quality. He achieves this in some of the more dramatic cards, such as the Chariot, who towers over his horses. He holds a melting shield displaying an upside-down snake. Death wears a tattered cloak, while worms slide from his skull. The blank-eyed angel in Judgement blows a horn over bramble-covered tombstones, one of them with a crude picture of a ship.

Unfortunately, the decision to distort the bodies gives the cards a strangeness that may repel rather than attract. The figures appear balloon-like, with huge shoulders and puffy arms.

The deck includes many comical touches. The High Priestess holds a mouse, as if about to feed her familiar, the cat. Both the Emperor and the Hierophant have ribbons in their beards. The Hierophant's beard also contains a bird's nest, as if he's forgotten to clean it, while his painted-on boots and tights remind us of comic-book super-heroes. In Strength a circus strongman bursts up out of the ground like a volcano to tear a book in half.

The court cards show static figures, in fixed positions. The bodies have the same distorted quality.

The suit cards depict the emblems (a kind of barber pole for the Wand) surrounding a simple central image.

The pattern of the Swords in the Five suggests an upside-down pentacle (the

KING OF CUPS

QUEEN OF BATONS

KNIGHT OF SWORDS

VI

VII

IIII

opposite of the pentacle for the Star, or Coin, cards). This suggests the confusion (and slander) of Witches as Satanists. As a rule, however, the deck avoids such implications.

The Prediction Tarot

This deck, designed by Bernard Stringer and illustrated by Peter Richardson, was created to go along with the book *Fortune-Telling By Tarot Cards*, written by Sasha Fenton. The designers have sought to create a beginner's deck, with clear and simple meanings. The booklet gives no descriptions of the cards, either artistic or spiritual. It only lists their use in readings. The realistic style of the deck, together with an original and often dramatic sense of design, seems to go beyond its 'official' purpose.

The Fool depicts a tramp, but a more modern and realistic one than we see in most decks. He stands under an arch within a frame, something we see in many of the other trumps, such as the Hierophant. This gives a sense of theatre to the cards. The Fool also resembles a master of ceremonies in the circus, with his red coat and what appears to be a whip. He might be announcing the drama of the Tarot, and yet, he remains a tramp, with his bag on a stick at his feet.

The Magician too appears more realistic and yet more mysterious than many traditional versions. We see a dark and cunning figure, a suggestion of a true medieval magician, a conjuror who creates for us this illusory tale of a soul's progress. He is the only character we see indoors.

The designs for many of the pictures imply new meanings. Instead of its usual stately progress or motionless stance, the Chariot hurtles along a cliff edge, suggesting recklessness and excitement much more than victory. In Temperance we find only the hint of the usual angel pouring water between two symbolic chalices. Clouds behind the woman suggest wings, but more as a hidden mystery. She reminds us of the biblical story of Rachel drawing water at the well.

In Judgement we see another dramatic change. Usually, the angel's blast brings forth a family – mother, father, baby, with the child's back to us. Here, startling the other two figures, we see a woman with a masculine face. She may be the same person as the dancer on the World.

Many of the cards appear in clouds or on mountain-tops, giving them a remote, dreamlike quality, which the realistic style only increases. Several go back to older, pre-esoteric images. The Wheel of Fortune takes away the Egyptian mythological animals and returns to the medieval moral lesson of rise and fall. At the same time, we see the evocative image of a woman cranking the Wheel (similar to the Simplified Tarot). We can describe her as the Goddess Fortuna, but what does it suggest that she wears a blindfold? Instead of the usual beatific vision for the Hanged Man we find a tramp staring with anguish at the money falling from his pockets.

The court cards are plain, without setting or symbolic ideas. The pip cards, especially the Swords and Staves, mimic elegant

designs of decks from the last century. They would probably satisfy the needs of fortune-telling, but they lack the suggestiveness of the trumps.

KING OF COINS

PAGE OF COINS

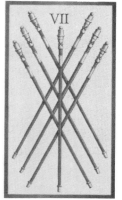

Hanson-Roberts Tarot

The Waite-Smith Rider pack changed the entire development of Tarot with its action

scenes on the Minor cards. A number of decks have achieved popularity by following

  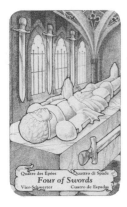 

Smith's example. Usually, they have followed her very closely, simply redoing the same scenes in their own style. Among the more elegant of these decks was the Aquarian Tarot of David Palladini, published in 1970. Recently, artists have begun to rethink the suit cards, though many will still base at least some of their cards on Smith (see Mother-peace and the Native American as examples, pp. 85, 110). Mary Hanson-Roberts has gone in the other direction. She has done her deck as a homage to Pamela Smith's designs, bringing to them a more dynamic draftsmanship, a use of close-ups and unusual angles, and more intense action.

The deck has proven quite popular, partly I suspect because people recognize the Smith scenes and feel comfortable with them at the same time that they like this more modern version.

Interestingly, we can also detect the influence of the Aquarian Tarot in this deck. The face of the Charioteer resembles some

of Palladini's characters, while the more flowering Rods refer to the Aquarian rather than the Rider pack. Hanson-Roberts, like Palladini, uses the term 'Rods' instead of 'Wands'.

We can find hints of other influences in some of the cards. The Chariot displays a yin-yang symbol rather than the lingam and yoni on the Rider pack Chariot. This suggests a change in cultural fashions, for in 1910 Hindu ideas greatly influenced occultists, while since then Taoism has become more popular. The Hierophant wears the triple crown and gives the Christian blessing. His clothes, however, and the designs on his keys, suggest Celtic Paganism. Behind him, instead of the columns of the Church, we see standing stones, with the kind of carvings found in Brittany and other Celtic lands. Death shows the Rider pack's armoured horseman, along with the king, maiden, and child. Here, however, all three lie dead, changing the symbolic implications even while it renders the scene more dramatic. The Lovers and the World Dancer are clothed, perhaps from a reluctance to show genitals or breasts.

As noted, the Minor cards follow Smith very closely. Still, the artist has changed some designs, as well as giving all of them her own quality. The Seven of Cups appears magical and fairy-like rather than signifying illusions. The Ace of Cups loses its overt Christian symbolism. Both the Ten and the Nine of Pentacles have become gentler and more cosy. On the Ten, instead of the isolated figures, all not looking at each other, we see a loving family with white-haired

grandpa, adoring child, and pooch. On the Nine, in place of the dignified woman with her trained falcon, we find a slightly simpering girl with her pet bird. Obviously, there is nothing wrong with changing the Rider pack images and meanings. However, ideally they should be changed to something of equal value. The change here results in little more than sweetness.

We might think of this deck as a children's Tarot. A number of the figures, such as the Queen of Cups, or the man in the Seven of Rods, appear a little like children dressed up as adults.

For myself, the biggest problem with this deck is a tendency to a sugary niceness. In such cards as the Fool, the Sun, and the Queen of Rods, we find the kind of pictures one sees on greeting cards for little girls.

The Queen of Rods is another child playing adult. Where the Rider pack gave her a black cat as a familiar the Hanson-Roberts version shows a sweet pussy-cat curled up in her lap (though out of proportion, for the cat is too large). Possibly this softness and sentimentality have contributed to the deck's success. I would like to think it comes more from the artist's sense of drama and action.

Sacred Rose Tarot

Johanna Gargiulo-Sherman, creator of the Sacred Rose Tarot, writes that her inspiration comes from medieval stained-glass windows, Byzantine icons, and the pre-Christian religion of nature. We can see these quite readily in the deck, with its deep colours, its posed

figures, and especially the thick trees with their overgrown foliage surrounding the people, giving the scenes an almost claustrophobic feeling of deep in an ancient wood.

The designs contain a tense energy between the figures. In Judgement the angel bears down on the people. In the World the four symbolic figures impinge on the dancing woman. The cards lack the stateliness of some earlier decks, but many people will find they make up for it in intensity. Others may find them too excessive, particularly in such voluptuous figures as the Lovers.

If Sherman has developed a Pagan imagery she also works with a set of symbols – an iconography – more related to Christian and Hermetic traditions. Red in the deck means passion and creativity, white purity and intuition. Feminine imagery indicates spiritual and lunar qualities, while masculine is physical and solar. These points will seem familiar, even basic to people with some knowledge of Tarot. It is worth pointing out that tradition assigns spirituality to the solar male and physicality to the lunar female. The symbolism becomes more specific with the rose, which Sherman describes as a Western equivalent of the Eastern lotus.

The back of the card presents a pattern of five roses, for the Major Arcana and the four suits of the Minor. In the centre the 'cosmic' symbolizes time and space, the Major Arcana. An aspect of this rose appears at the bottom of each of the trumps, most clearly in the Fool. The red rose represents sacrifice and the suit of Wands. The white means purity and Cups. The blue signifies 'the

Nine of Swords

Six of Swords

Seven of Wands

Five of Wands

Knight of Wands

0 ◄ The Fool

impossible', linked with Swords, while gold, for Pentacles, means 'absolute achievement'.

Sherman refers to the various trees on the cards as the Tree of Life. Many people will know this term from Kabbalah and may expect to see those symbols in the cards.

However, the tree here is not an abstract form, but a living plant. It reminds us that the intellectual tree of the Kabbalists comes from an older, nature-based religion.

Sherman writes that she wanted her cards to convey a direct meaning. A person with no knowledge of Tarot ideas should experience joy in the Fool and wisdom in the High Priestess. Probably no artist can do this. In Tarot classes I have noticed that when people look at cards spontaneously, without formal knowledge of the pictures, any and all meanings become assigned to particular cards. Sherman, however, does not depend only on emotional reactions. The cards con-
ceal precise meanings. The Hierophant's triple cross is said to have seven bars, for the seven planetary virtues and vices.

The Minor cards include original, sometimes partly abstract designs, such as the frightening Nine of Swords. Other cards derive from Pamela Smith, but with a more dramatic form, as in the Six of Swords. Again, some people will find these exciting, while others will consider them excessive. The Seven and five of Wands resemble comic-book super-heroes. A few cards, particularly the Knight of Wands, recall the Frieda Harris paintings for Aleister Crowley's Book of Thoth.

CHAPTER 3
Story-telling Tarots

In the esoteric interpretation of the Tarot, the cards function as symbols, almost abstractions (the Hanged Man reduces to a figure 4 over a triangle). And yet, the Major Arcana have always shown people, and to some extent, actions. If we put aside the Hanged Man's *meaning* we can wonder how this person got into this situation. We can view the Moon as a landscape with beasts howling in the night. In short, each card has always represented a moment in a story.

As people have begun to re-imagine the Tarot, a number of artists have created decks in precisely this way – not as a spiritual philosophy, or cultural tableaux, or a way of creating a new consciousness, but as a collection of frozen moments in somebody's story. Instead of showing formally posed figures, they give us actions, a witch casting a spell, a frightened poet lost in the woods, a woman and a monster dancing together in a labyrinth. Often they will link this approach to some other purpose. The Merlin Tarot seeks to give us a sense of the esoteric truths in British native tradition; but it also sees these truths as emerging through traditions of story-telling. The Dante Tarot wishes to explore meanings and structures within the work of the great Italian poet. The Minotarot and the Mythic Tarot both draw on Greek mythology as a way of exploring psychological mysteries; the Mythic does this through retelling the primary myths in pictures, while the Minotarot plays with one special story, turning it into a dream of sex, violence,

mystery, and delight. The Tarots of Elisabetta Cassari, as well as the Tarot of the Cat People, differ from the others by discarding almost all concerns other than story. The Cat People creates a science fiction fantasy. Cassari's work shows little or no interest in symbolism. She develops themes of politics and magic, but always through characters and dramatic action.

Most decks come with a text explaining the pictures. The Minotarot gives us a few words, the Mythic a complete tale. And yet, the pictures exist independent of the explanations. Juliet Sharman-Burke and Liz Greene may tell us that the Seven of Swords shows Orestes sneaking into the castle at Argos. But the picture shows only a hooded figure carrying seven swords at night. Whole ranges of stories become possible when we look at the picture as a fresh image.

In his book *The Castle of Crossed Destinies* Italo Calvino explored this use of the Tarot. A group of travellers find themselves stranded in a castle. A spell prevents any of them from speaking. To tell their stories each one in turn uses Tarot cards. Each assembles a particular set of cards and turns them over one by one, showing the events of his life. What the narrator does not say is that we do not get the characters' actual stories, but rather the narrator's *assumption* of those stories. That is, the narrator says a certain card refers to an event; in fact, he makes the event up, for he cannot know what meaning the person actually intends. Calvino used the Tarot as a metaphor for the gulf that exists between the teller and the listener. The story is meant to bridge that gulf, but for both it actually opens to a different world. At the same time, Calvino expressed his fascination with the Tarot as pure images, calling the cards 'a machine for telling stories'.

Calvino's experiment – and the experiments of the Minotarot, which gives the barest meanings – open up possibilities for 'reading' the cards in a new way. Instead of interpreting the pictures as events or objective states, we can make up a story with whatever cards we happen to choose. This story would tell us something about ourselves, but in a more intimate, more genuinely revelatory way, for it would not attempt to say, 'Your girl friend does not love you, but you will soon meet someone else for a true romance', but rather give the person an opportunity to discover what kind of tale she or he can create with images of sorrow and love.

One problem with such a reading is that each deck carries its own biases. With the Cassari decks, for example, it becomes difficult to create a story that does not deal with oppression, sorcery, violence, and revenge. The vividness of the Dante Tarot exposes our imaginations to the subjects and beliefs of Dante and the deck's creator. And yet, any form of reading – or meditation, or study – with the Tarot aligns us with the deck's particular biases. For storytelling as with any other use of the cards, we have the option of choosing the deck we like and the requirement of understanding its inherent attitudes and messages.

The decks in this section tell stories as their primary purpose. The also allow us to recognize storytelling as a possibility for a great many modern decks, including many of the cultural Tarots, the women's Tarots, and a number of the popular decks.

The Tarots of Elisabetta Cassari

Elisabetta Cassari has (at this writing) done three decks for the Solleone card company of Milan, Italy. The first of these, known as the Solleone Tarot, was the first contemporary deck commissioned by the Italian publisher Vito Arienti.

After the Solleone Tarot, Cassari went on to create the Future Solleone, a deck which

makes the story-telling theme even more explicit, by setting the cards in a kind of science fiction/fantasy epic. We can describe them as influenced by myth, fairy-tales, and Hollywood movies such as *Star Wars*. The third deck is a limited edition of 22 black and white 'arcani'. Showing scenes of torture and injustice, these cards emphasize Cassari's

THE DEVIL

THE STAR

THE MOON

attention to political oppression mixed with fantastic imagery.

The original Solleone Tarot is possibly the first deck with storytelling as its main theme. Cassari has described it as a 'poetic story with messages of hope and love, despite images shrouded' by the heavy burdens of daily life. Each card shows an action, an event, or a character in a story. For the Devil, instead of the usual Pan or Baphomet of occult decks, we find Mephistopheles buying the soul of a scholar (Faust?). In the Star we find a Renaissance astronomer, and in the Moon a woman on a fantasy bird.

With some of her pictures Cassari stays relatively close to the tradition, at the same time distorting them for her own purposes. La Papessa shows the female pope sitting in a chair with a suggestion of a veil behind her. But she is scheming and wicked, a sorceress rather than a keeper of truth. Other cards, such as The Lover or The Chariot, disregard the usual images entirely.

The Chariot, along with The Pope, helps her develop a satirical portrait of the corrupt Church, a familiar theme among many Italian decks. Notice the hypocrisy of the Pope's and cardinal's gestures of benediction.

A number of people have recoiled from the violence in these cards. Some time ago I mentioned the Solleone Tarot to a friend of mine who had studied and written about the Tarot. He thought a moment and then said, 'Oh, that's the one where everyone gets hacked to pieces.' Violence is certainly prominent in these decks. Strength, the Hanged Man and Judgement, three cards which usually

show transfiguration, here become scenes of torture or murder.

Other cards, such as Temperance, become changed to scenes opposite to their original meaning. In Temperance we see excess, the greed of the rich, while the jester, symbolizing the poor, must fight with the animals for his scraps of food. Cassari has discarded the usual occult or religious themes. Her deck is frankly political. In Judgement we see an implied story, a village witch sentenced to burn at the stake for refusing to submit to the Inquisition. If it shows pain, it also shows courage. Above all, it shows a story.

Witches are very prominent in these cards. Interestingly, they tend to appear as evil sorceresses in the trumps, and courageous peasant women in the Minor cards. Probably this derives from identifying the Major cards with the ruling classes.

THE EMPRESS

Seven of Wands

Two of Wands

In the Empress we see a sorceress queen, reminiscent of the evil ruler in Disney's version of *Snow White*. The Seven of Wands, on the other hand, shows a heroic barefoot woman casting a spell against evil. She, like the 'band of witches' (Stuart Kaplan's expression) of the Two of Wands, seeks to defend her people against oppression.

Notice the fantasy creature in the Empress.

Part bird and part lizard, with a human head, it suggests enchantment (in fact, all the trumps show some sort of impossible beast). Kaplan describes it as once a man, now enslaved by its own evil and the Empress's spells.

The Court cards are not symbolic figures or psychological portraits, but characters. We see the Queen of Cups dancing under

Queen of Cups

Queen of Swords

Page of Pentacles

Asso di Bastoni / Ace of Wands

Dieci di Coppe / Ten of Cups

Asso di Spade / Ace of Swords

Cinque di Denari / Five of Pentacles

the full Moon, the Queen of Swords a triumphant Bedouin who has killed a knight with his own sword, the Page of Coins a penniless student.

The Wands cards appear more balanced than the trumps, less violent. This is because they depict the peasants, the heroes of the Solleone Tarot. The Cups show women in all facets, from witches to harried house-wives. The Swords return us to the violence of the trumps, including the horrendous Ace of Swords, while the Coins bring us gamblers, prostitutes, misers, and corrupt judges.

In the 'Gli Arcani di Elisabetta' we find the same themes and similar images as the original Solleone deck. In the series Chariot, Justice, and Hermit we find the three basic ideas.

Il Carro 7

La Giustizia 8

L'Eremita 9

La Luna 18

Instead of a triumphant hero, the Chariot shows a victim, a bound figure in a box, or a cart on the way to an execution. Instruments of torture reach out to him. Justice also reverses the usual spiritual concept by showing temporal injustice, in the form of the Church. The Hermit is yet another form of reversal. Not a wise male who stands on a mountain-top, removed from human weak-

ness, but a woman in a cave, a witch stirring her magic cauldron. We can think of her as stirring up trouble, or as casting a spell against the evil and injustice shown in the other cards. Witches and sorceresses allow Cassari to work with the traditional elements of European storytelling. In the Moon, the witch rides on a broom. Naked and wrinkled, but also muscular, she has an untamed

La Papessa   2

L'Imperatrice   3

L'Imperatore   4

Il Papa   5

power. There is a suggestion of horns in the sky, implying the Devil, and yet we cannot say for sure that she represents evil, for she lacks the corruption of such figures as the Empress.

For the ruling class, power becomes evil. In the quartet of the Papess, the Empress, the Emperor, and the Pope, we see a gallery of degenerate rulers. The Pope in particular appears depraved, his eyes unfocused, his hands almost trembling.

Even more than in the first deck, we find an obsession with torture, and a deeply pessimistic view of humanity. Temperance shows force-feeding, Judgement once again depicts a woman burning at the stake – though here we do not see her heroically resisting; she only waits for the fire. For the World we find a public execution. The Fool carries a certain glee in its transformation of a human into a donkey.

La Temperanza 14

Il Giudizio   20

Il Mondo   21

Il Pazzo   0

At first glance the Future Solleone would appear to be an SF version of the original Cassari deck. In fact, these cards go beyond the first deck in both style and content. The pictures are rougher, but at the same time

with more depth and suggestiveness. We see this very strikingly in the first trump, Il Caos. Cassari has also given much freer rein to her imagination. Card four, Uccelli E Pesci, expresses her delight in fantasy beasts in a

UCCELLI E PESCI

LA LUCE

IL CAOS

IL PAZZO

1 - STANZA

TERRA

way that the more traditional cards made impossible.

Spacemen and robots are to this deck what witches and demons are to the Solleone. They represent basic conventions of SF story-telling. The bored, down-and-out spaceman of one Terra (Ace of Staves) has become a stock figure in SF stories. Twenty-two, Il Pazzo, suggests the Fool-like hero of Isaac Asimov's *Foundation* series. This is probably not intended, but it also is not an accident, for Cassari deals here in the basic images that give SF its power.

We see no attempt to depict accurate technology or future conditions. Despite its title, the deck concerns itself more with myth than the future. We see this very clearly in the first card, Il Caos, an image of the origins of life. While card two, La Luce, introduces the spaceman, the sequence reminds us of the Bible and other creation stories, in which light penetrates the dark chaos before the beginning.

By setting her deck in the future, Cassari gives herself the freedom to depart whenever she likes from the normal Tarot designations. Eighteen, the comic image of aliens marrying before a computer instead of a priest,

IL MATRIMONIO

LA GIUSTIZIA

LA MORTE

1 - NASCITA

FUOCO

1 - CONCEPIMENTO

ACQUA

1 - FAMILIA

ARIA

resembles the Moon only if we see the aliens as the dog and wolf.

Some cards stay with the original names and/or subjects. Eight, La Forza, shows the same abuse of power as the other decks. La Morte, however, card thirteen, gives us an image of the human spirit liberated from the machine-like shell of the spaceman.

The Minor cards use the four elements rather than the symbols. They give us four realms, a cave-like world of semi-apemen for Fuoco (Fire), an underwater kingdom for Acqua (Water), space for Aria (Air), and a worn-out poverty-stricken Earth for Terra. They are all stock images of SF, found in

Hollywood B movies as well as serious SF novels.

The themes for each card seem to have little to do with the subjects developed by the Golden Dawn and now considered traditional.

In most decks the five of Cups depicts loss. Here we see a monster bringing death. The eight of Swords normally shows bondage (a favourite theme of Cassari's). Here we find happiness, a figure rejoicing in space. The three of Pentacles usually shows artistic mastery. Here we find an SF version of the Faust legend. This last card makes explicit an underlying theme of machines as corrupt.

5 - MORTE

ACQUA

8 - FELICITÀ

ARIA

3 - CONTRATTO

TERRA

The Tarot of the Cat People

Like the Future Solleone Tarot, this deck joins the Tarot to SF. Karen Kuykendall's

connection to SF is more intimate, for she has worked as a SF illustrator, and clearly sees

VII The Chariot

XIV Temperance

Nine of Swords

Eight of Swords

Seven of Wands

as SF. In her instruction booklet Kuykendall tells us that the people of her world must go to great lengths to earn the respect of cats. While many people, including myself, will find all this sentimental and kitschy, the deck has proved popular. We should also recognize that the deck as a whole takes the story approach to Tarot further than Cassari's cards. She sets her scenes in a specific fantasy world called 'The Outer Regions', with five kingdoms. Kuykendall apparently is writing a book based on the cards and their story lines.

And yet, the cards themselves show little re-imagination other than adding flowing costumes and cats on every card.
The trumps are pared down versions of traditional cards. Many of the Minor cards show little more than someone posing amongst a variety of cats. And while some of the cats have a stylized quality, like those of the High Priestess or the Emperor, many, such as those on the Ten of Swords or The Lovers, appear overly cute, more like the pictures on greeting cards than real cats.

her deck as a coherent SF world. She also shows an emotional attachment to her world which we could hardly imagine with Cassari's ironic (and violent) images. In an introduction, Stuart Kaplan comments that Kuykendall attends SF conventions dressed in the flowing costumes shown in her deck. The inspiration for the cards comes from her own love of cats – she lives with ten – as well

II The High Priestess

IV The Emperor

Ten of Swords

VI The Lovers

0 The Fool

V The High Priest

Ace of Swords

The Five Kingdoms are entirely fantasy. At the same time the pictures show certain cultural influences. The Fool, and perhaps The Lovers, appear somewhat Japanese, the High Priest carries a suggestion of Aztec or other Central American Indians, and the Ace of Swords resembles an African warrior.

Kuykendall lives in the Arizona desert. Her love for this land comes through in her description of the Outer Regions. She describes the 'awesome silence', and the way

the ' "ping" of tiny grains of sand bouncing on soft air currents over the slickrock . . . can be heard for miles.'

The deck seems a curious mixture of seriousness and sentimentality. Kuykendall has worked hard to develop a concept of a world, and yet the cards themselves do not really convey it, for the pictures remain static. They are too posed, too lacking in event, to carry us into the fantasies Kuykendall intends to create.

The Mythic Tarot

The Mythic Tarot was designed by Tarot writer Juliet Sharman-Burke and astrologer/psychologist Liz Greene. Tricia Newell painted the cards. Despite Greene's influence, the text makes no attempt to connect the

THE FOOL

THE EMPRESS

cards to astrology. The deck comes in a package with a book by Sharman-Burke and Greene.

The Mythic Tarot introduces us to Greek mythology. Unfortunately, some of the pictures have turned out overly sweet, tending toward kitsch, a quality not found at all in Greek mythology. The Fool depicts Dionysus, God of ecstasy and rebirth. The Empress shows us Demeter, The Great Mother. The figures on both cards appear pretty, with somewhat simpering smiles and rosy cheeks.

The trumps show characters and events in the Greek pantheon. The Emperor shows Zeus atop Mt Olympus, Strength (number Eight, as in the Golden Dawn) shows Heracles killing the Nemean lion, and the Lovers depicts the judgement of Paris, the beginning of the Trojan War.

In the Minor cards the storytelling aspect of the deck becomes even more specific. Each suit describes a specific story from Greek myth. Cups shows us the tale of Eros and Psyche, Wands that of Jason and the Golden Fleece, Swords the monstrous story of Orestes, and Pentacles the life of Daedalus the inventor. The deck's creators have chosen the subjects to match the traditional quality of the suit. The choices demonstrate a great seriousness in this deck, for the story of Orestes, who must kill his mother to avenge his father, and who then is driven mad by the Furies, is a very harsh tale, matching the story of Oedipus in its ability to show us sides of ourselves we might prefer not to recognize.

The numbered cards in the suit tell the story in sequence, beginning, however, with the Two. Just as in many decks the Aces link the suits to the Major Arcana, so here the Aces show Goddesses and Gods who figure prominently in the particular story of the suit. They are, in fact, 'the initiator and moving power behind the tale', as the text says of Zeus and the Golden Fleece.

For Cups we see Aphrodite, mother of Eros and tester of Psyche. Wands shows us Zeus with the Golden Fleece (for the ram was given to him in sacrifice). The Ace of Swords depicts Athena, redeemer of Orestes (the Goddess of Wisdom, she appears more often in the deck than any other character). For Pentacles we see Poseidon, whose white bull fathered the Minotaur.

The court cards give us characters who are also meant to represent personality types. This is the traditional divinatory approach to court cards. Sometimes these characters are peripheral figures from the story shown in the suit. The Page of Wands shows Phrixus who originally flew on the golden ram to

PAGE OF WANDS

KING OF CUPS

QUEEN OF PENTACLES

TWO OF CUPS

THREE OF CUPS

FOUR OF CUPS

FIVE OF CUPS

Colchis. Other figures simply reflect the necessary qualities for the card. The King of Cups is Orpheus, meant to show the 'active, dynamic dimension of water'. The Queen of Pentacles is Omphale, another lesser figure, who appears in the tale of Heracles.

The suits tell their stories vividly. In Cups, for instance, if we did not know the story of Eros and Psyche we could almost work it out from the pictures. More significantly, anyone who did know the tale would recognize it immediately from the first scenes.

In Wands and Swords we find the same clarity. We need only glance at the Two and Five of Wands to know that the suit depicts Jason seeking the fleece. The Three and

TWO OF WANDS

FIVE OF WANDS

THREE OF SWORDS

NINE OF SWORDS

Nine of Swords tell us immediately that we are seeing the agony of Orestes. Interestingly, while the Three gives us Agamemnon murdered in his bath, the suit avoids showing us the central event, Orestes' murder of his mother.

Only in the suit of Pentacles does the deck lose some of its ability to carry a story. While the Seven might give us a clue that we are seeing Daedalus with Pasiphae, such cards as the Eight, Nine, and Ten tell us very little. Oddly, the deck omits all three of the most famous images from this particular story. We

do not find the labyrinth, or the Minotaur, or the winged flight of Daedalus and Icarus.

The choice of Greek mythology for these cards comes from two connected ideas. First, Sharman-Burke and Greene believe that Greek mythology contains such variety that it shows all of life, at both actual and psychological levels. Second, they see Greek mythology as the source of Western European culture and therefore of particular relevance to the Tarot. While no one could doubt the depth and variety of Greek mythology, we might question its universality. For one thing, polytheism implies a particular outlook on the world. It differs sharply from monotheism, as well as from the atheism of followers of the Tao, or the personal vision of some Native American religions. Furthermore, Greek myth contains biases, notably an emphasis on violence and explosions of repressed sexuality. The book for the Mythic Tarot sometimes gives the impression of the human psyche as filled with dark secrets. This view may come in part from dwelling on the particular obsessions of the ancient Greeks.

We might also question the importance of Greek mythology for modern seekers of the mythic experience. Without a Classical education, most people know little of Greek myth. In the United States, Native American religions have become much more central, while in Western Europe the Native traditions of the Celts and the Scandinavians have gone through another of their cyclic revivals. Finally, the Tarot has become so bound up with Kabbalist and Hermetic imagery it becomes very difficult to shift the cards so totally to another area. What the cards do demonstrate is the possibility of using Tarot forms to portray powerful stories.

The Minotarot

With this unusual Tarot we again enter Greek mythology. This time, however, we deal with only one story, and in fact a small part of that story. At first glance, this deck seems very limited. There are only two settings for the pictures: outside and inside the labyrinth. There are only four characters: Theseus, Ariadne, the Minotaur, and the Minotauress, the last an invention of Provoost, the deck's creator. The story itself

appears to go nowhere, or rather to loop back on itself. Characters die in one card and come back to life in another. They fight and then embrace, lovers switch partners, sorrow turns to joy and back to sorrow.

The deck only begins to make sense when we think of it as a dream. In dreams events happen as they will, according to shifts of energy in the unconscious. Dream logic is associative rather than cause and effect. One

thing suggests another, often its reversal.

Greek myth is extremely complicated, with stories moving in and out of each other. The myth of Theseus contains many incidents, with the labyrinth only one of them, while the labyrinth story itself goes back before the birth of the Minotaur. The Minotarot narrows the material down to its essentials – and then pays little attention to the original accounts. Like a number of other twentieth-century artists, Provoost sees the labyrinth as a metaphor for the twisting darknesses of the subconscious, with its 'polymorphous perverse' sexuality, its secret love of violence, its jealousy and desire for betrayal. Observe the astonishing sequence 26–30 (all trumps, by the way).

Here are Provoost's descriptions:

26   TEMPERANCE   Theseus is seduced by the Minotaur
27   DEATH   The   Minotaur   slays Theseus
28   THE   DEVIL   Theseus   slays   the Minotauress
29   THE   LOVERS   Theseus   and   the Minotauress fall in love
30   STRENGTH   The Minotauress kills Theseus

Chute

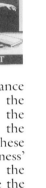

LE JUGEMENT

Eclaircissement

Allegresse

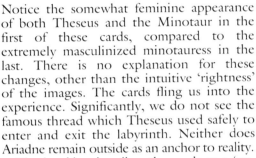

Notice the somewhat feminine appearance of both Theseus and the Minotaur in the first of these cards, compared to the extremely masculinized minotauress in the last. There is no explanation for these changes, other than the intuitive 'rightness' of the images. The cards fling us into the experience. Significantly, we do not see the famous thread which Theseus used safely to enter and exit the labyrinth. Neither does Ariadne remain outside as an anchor to reality.

The booklet describes the cards as a 'traditional Tarot'. Strictly speaking, this is so, for we find twenty-two trump cards and four suits with fourteen cards each, including four labelled as court cards. The order of the cards and even the distinction between the suits is of no importance. What matters is the number on the upper right – the place where that card comes in the sequence of the myth.

In a number of cards we see the image of someone falling into or emerging from a hole. They suggest yet a further descent, into a dark mystery beyond even the dream world of the labyrinth. Notice in 77 the joy of Theseus and Ariadne as they both emerge at last from the Underworld. Notice as well the streaks of light in the 'sky' on 73, 76, and 77. Such images appear on many of the cards, sometimes abstract, sometimes suggesting objects, such as an eye on 73 and a bird on 77.

The author of the booklet (presumably Provoost) has devised a special 'fortune-telling' technique. The method involves 'following the thread of one of the possible stories' in the deck. The person mixes the cards and chooses one. Then the reader looks at a table in the booklet and sees the choice of cards to follow this one. For instance, if you choose card 18, this gives you a choice of 20, 21, 22, or 24 as the next card. If you choose 21, this tells you to go to 25, 26, or 27. To ensure randomness, a reader could present the choices face down and ask the questioner to choose one of the cards. Some cards call for only one possible follow card. Others have no following cards at all. These would then form the end of the story. You can also stop at any point when the story seems to have reached a proper conclusion. When the person has chosen the cards and laid out the tale, he or she can then make up his or her own story from the pictures, a story which may reflect the person's life, or simply lead to an understanding more connected to the psyche than to outside events. When I described this method to a friend of mine she pointed out that such a reading frees the cards from the issue of how 'true' they are, that is, how much they correspond with external situations.

The Minotarot works from a very limited vocabulary. Instead of closing down possibilities, the narrow range opens them up. It demands that we engage our own imagination with the pictures. More than most other new decks it follows the implications of Tarot as myth, a possibility long neglected.

The Dante Tarot

This remarkable deck, created by Lise Guemoud-Moudz, gives pictorial form to the works of Dante Alighieri. Though the earliest Tarots did not appear until more than a century after Dante wrote *The Divine Comedy*, they do come out of the same culture. In creating her deck, Guemoud-Moudz has followed certain interpretations of Dante, especially *Il linguaggio segreto di Dante e dei 'Fedeli d' Amore* by Luigi Valli, and *L'esoterismo di Dante* by René Guenon. The full name for the deck is I Tarocchi Di Dante e Dei Fedeli D'Amore.

Many people have illustrated the *Commedia*, or done paintings based on scenes. Usually they have attempted to capture its grandeur and sweep. Guemoud-Moudz has taken a much more intimate approach, showing us individual characters and events. She makes us realize that the Tarot, for all its spiritual philosophy, speaks to us in an intimate way, with images that become personal as well as mysterious.

The cards do not simply illustrate Dante's works; they interpret them. The range across all of the poet's writings, though the most references belong to the *Commedia*. Most cards, at least in the Major Arcana, do not show a particular scene, but rather refer to two or more points in the work. The Two of spades refers to no less than seven texts. As a simple example of her combination of

the cards and the works, we can look at the Magician. We see the usual figure before a table with various implements. Set into the wood frame above him we see the lemniscate (infinity sign). Even without the title and the number most people would recognize the Magician. And yet, by showing him writing, the card clearly depicts Dante himself. For reference the artist has chosen two short passages from the *Purgatorio*. XIV 20–1 reads, 'there is no point in telling you my name,/for I have not as yet won fame on Earth' (translation, Mark Musa, Penguin books). This gives us the poet's comment on his condition in society, as well as his confidence in eventual fame. The second passage is not so obvious. XXXI 55 reads 'When you first felt deception's arrow sting'. Beatrice has just appeared in the previous canto, replacing Virgil as the poet's guide. She attacks Dante for worldly concerns. The line refers to her own death, when Dante should have realized the impermanence of physical attractions. His thoughts should have followed her to heaven, rather than remaining in the world. In a sense, the first reference characterizes the poet, while the second criticizes that very concern for fame. We see here the complex relationship between the pictures and the texts. The poems illustrate the picture as much as the other way around.

Seven cards do not refer at all to Dante's

writings. Six of them show biblical scenes. The text for the Knight of Cups, whose text quotes Wolfram von Eschenbach, thereby linking the card – and the suit – specifically to the Holy Grail.

In the Major Aracana the artist faced a traditional set of Tarot images. Some of these she adapts very closely, such as the Papess or the Tower. Others refer more closely to the poems, such as the Star and the Moon.

While a standard image, the Papess also depicts Beatrice, Dante's great inspiration. The references for the Tower include *Purgatorio* XXVI, which describes the sinners of Sodom, destroyed by fire and brimstone. The specific line, 82, reads 'and ours was an hermaphroditic sin'. In the Tarot the crowned hermaphrodite is a positive image.

The Star appears to show Beatrice flying with Dante. The references include the last line of both the *Inferno* and the *Purgatorio*: 'and we came out once more to see the stars,' and 'eager to rise, now ready for the stars'. The final reference, however, becomes more complex. *Paradiso* XXXII, 145 reads 'But lest you fall backwards beating your wings', and tells the pilgrim he must not depend on his vision alone, but must ascend to heaven through prayer.

The Moon would appear to illustrate the famous opening, with Dante lost in the deep woods at night; the references do include *Inferno* I. The text, however, also refers to *Inferno* XX 127–9 'and the moon last night already was at full;/and you should well remember that at times/when you were lost

in the dark wood she helped you.'

The Fool demonstrates the complexity of the deck, and the way the artist allows herself to make changes. It refers to the first canto, in which a leopard, a lion, and a hungry she-wolf block the pilgrim's path. *Inferno* II 120 also refers to the beast 'blocking the quick way up the mount of bliss'. The picture, however, shows a dog as well as the three wild animals. It also depicts the pilgrim walking up stairs to a door rather than being blocked from climbing a mountain. A third reference sends us to *Purgatorio* II 46, which quotes Psalm 113, 'In exitu Israel de Aegypto'. This seems a curious source. However, the liberation of Israel forms a central motif for the soul's journey of liberation in the *Commedia*. And the soul's liberation forms the theme of the Fools's journey through the Major Arcana. In the poem, the characters sing this psalm on Easter morning,

in the year 1300. The Tarot commentary gives us the information that on that day the sun stood in 22 degrees Aries, and (if I understand the Italian correctly), when Dante leaves Purgatory, the Moon is crossing 22 degrees Libra. Twenty-two, of course, is the number of cards in the Major Arcana. Furthermore, in Dante's Epistle to Can Grande della Scala he describes the different levels at which one might interpret his great work. The biblical text he uses as an example begins with 'In exitu Israel de Aegypto'. And the four methods of approaching a text – literal, moral, allegorical, anagogical – can guide us through the Tarot as well as the *Commedia*. (See, in Esoteric Tarots, the Enoil Gavat and Stairs of Gold by Giorgio Tavaglione.)

The four suits display different classes of sins, while being interspersed with more holy images. Wands show cruelty, Swords war and treason, Coins greed, and Cups sins of the flesh. Some of the pictures, such as the Two of Wands and the Three of Coins, show grotesque or harsh images, capturing that aspect of Dante.

Other cards show the fantastic elements of Dante's imagination, as in the Ten of Wands. While maintaining the deck's intimate quality we get an epic sweep in such cards as the Six of Swords.

There are scenes from myth and history. The Nine of Swords shows Jason and the Golden Fleece (compare this with the Mythic Tarot), while the Ten of Swords depicts Caesar's assassination, an event of great importance in Dante's work (compare the Ten of Swords from Dali).

The artist has painted these scenes with great variety. The characters are stark and drawn with strength and physical presence. The colour tones are deep and vivid, with each of the Minor suits emphasizing a particular colour to match the element. The style manages the difficult feat of blending the modern and the medieval.

The Merlin Tarot

With its recreation of Celtic imagery and myth, this deck could easily belong with the Cultural Tarots. I have included it with Storytelling because of Stewart's own statements that he saw stories as a primary focus for the design. The 'story-telling tradition', rather than cosmology or 'morbid intellectual' symbolism, fired the creation of the deck. And yet, within that tradition, the deck is deeply symbolic. The Merlin Tarot shows us how esoteric meanings arise out of images.

Stewart based his concept for the deck on the *Vita Merlini*, a twelfth-century 'biography' of the wizard Merlin, written by Geoffrey of Monmouth, who also wrote *History of the Kings of Britain*, the earliest written source for many of the King Arthur legends. Stewart has explicated the *Vita* in his book, *The Mystic Life of Merlin*. In *The Mystic Life*, and in his description of the Merlin Tarot (not published at the time of this writing), Stewart has presented an argument for the Celtic esoteric system and the Tarot as expressions of a single tradition. Since the *Vita Merlini* predates the first Italian Tarots by more than two hundred years, Stewart's argument could greatly change our theories of the Tarot's origins.

To some extent, this involves matching images from two separate systems. That is, both the Tarot and Celtic myth present certain fundamental figures. These might include the ideas of magicians, mystical death, innocence, the elements, the importance of the Moon, Sun, and Stars, and so on. One scene from the *Vita Merlini* does stand out for its powerful connection to the Tarot's most mysterious image, the Hanged Man. Stewart titles this scene the Threefold Death, and maintains that the seemingly comic tale

VII FOOL XIII HANGED MAN

derives from 'extremely ancient' and secret initiations. Briefly, the story runs as follows. After a period as a hermit Merlin returns to court, where his magical sight reveals Queen Ganieda's infidelity. To reassure the king, Ganieda sets out to discredit Merlin (her brother) as a prophet. She spots a boy in court and brings him forward. How will he die? she asks Merlin. The seer says that the boy will fall from a high rock. Ganieda takes the boy away, disguises him, and brings him back. How will this boy die? Merlin says he will 'meet with a violent death in a tree.' Finally, Ganieda dresses the boy as a girl and brings him back. How will the girl die? 'Girl or not,' says Merlin, 'she shall die in the river.' The king laughs and forgives his wife. Later, the poem tells us, the boy, grown now, goes hunting. Chasing a stag, he falls off a precipice into a river. As he falls one of his feet catches in a tree. 'Thus he fell, and was drowned, and hung from a tree.'

XVII EMPEROR XXI PRIESTESS IV FORTUNE

Stewart rightly points out that hanging by one foot from a tree makes him the image of the Hanged Man. We can add, as well, that many esoteric decks add water underneath the Hanged Man, and that the more modern decks assign the card astrologically to Neptune.

Whatever judgement we make about Celtic tradition as the source of Tarot, the artist for the Merlin Tarot, Miranda Gray, has created a deck which brings to life the myths and artistic traditions of her sources. There is a fine sense of nature and the mystic connections of the soul to the land.

Several of the cards emphasize the mythic and the mysterious.

VI JUDGEMENT

XVI TEMPERANCE

XII DEATH

Judgement derives from *The Prophecies of Merlin*, which tells of a Goddess called Ariadne who unweaves the solar system, leaving only the four winds. Death shows us the Celtic 'Apple Woman'.

Some people might find the trump and court figures overly pretty, too tame and comfortable. One woman who saw the proofs with me said they reminded her of Beatrix Potter illustrations. We see this quality most in the Star, but also in other cards.

III STAR

BEASTS

BIRDS

BEASTS

ACE

Humour

ACE

Endurance

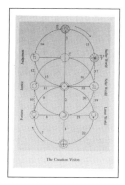

The Creation Vision

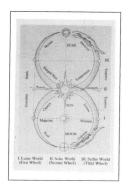

I Lunar World (First Wheel) II Solar World (Second Wheel) III Stellar World (Third Wheel)

The suit cards do not show scenes, but rather motifs from Celtic art. These match the four totems, Serpents, Fishes, Birds, Beasts. The Aces appear to be the artist's original designs.

The examples given for the trumps will have made clear that Stewart has drastically rearranged the numbering, as well as some of the names. The order follows a complex arrangement based on the creation vision of the bard Taliesin, described in the *Vita Merlini*. This vision appears in diagram form (different than the illustrations in Stewart's *The Mystic Life of Merlin*) on two extra cards, with the trumps shown in their places.

Notice, in these diagrams, the resemblance to the Kabbalist Tree of Life, with three vertical columns, ten positions, and a number of pathways linking the circles.

Stewart has indicated that he intends to use his deck for storytelling in a future book. It will be interesting to see what emerges from the images.

CHAPTER 4
Cultural Tarots

Different interpretations of the Tarot have always centered on the question of its origins. Did it begin as a game or an esoteric text? And if esoteric, what specific doctrine was it demonstrating? If people created decks using Egyptian imagery they justified it with the claim that the Tarot began in ancient Egypt. If they included Hebrew letters they did so from the belief that the Tarot represents a pictorial version of Kabbalah. In the past fifteen years, something new has come into Tarot design: a linking of the Tarot patterns with imagery and iconography of cultures making no claim at all on Tarot origins or tradition.

When Peter Balin created his Xultun Mayan Tarot he justified his use of South American imagery with the assumption that Tarot and Mayan mythology both derived from inherent structures in the cosmos and the human imagination. This essentially Platonic idea assumes that a basic grid of reality exists, an ideal which we never actually see, for only specific versions of it emerge, in different times and places. Therefore, Balin argues, the Tarot and Mayan religion represent the same thing, even if their original makers knew nothing about each other. And yet, it is also clear that Peter Balin simply wished to bring together two consuming interests of his own.

Later cultural Tarots have not found it necessary to give even this much justification. When Stuart Kaplan commissioned the Ukiyoe Tarot, he wanted only to join an art style he had long admired to the subject he knows best. The Native American Tarot presents itself primarily as a panorama of life among the original nations of North America. I have included two Egyptian based Tarots in this section, the Tarot of Transition and Egipcios Kier. I might also have included the Enoil Gavat Tarot, which uses Egyptian imagery. However, the Enoil Gavat uses an Egyptian *style*, while the others give us genuine Egyptian mythology and daily life.

As with artistic Tarots a number of these decks are esoteric. They come from designers who have followed some particular path of initiation and now wish to present that in the form of a Tarot. This may come from a stated or implicit belief that Tarot forms the essence of the Western Hermetic tradition, so that the use of Tibetan symbols in the Tarot trumps (as in the Kashmir Tarot) will best realize Tibetan ideas in a Western context.

Other decks carry a storytelling quality. I might just as well have included the Merlin Tarot in the cultural section, or the Norse Tarot in the storytelling. By choosing mythological characters and scenes, or situations from daily life, decks such as the Norse and the Ukiyoe lend themselves to spinning of tales. The Ukiyoe deck brings out Stuart Kaplan's own penchant for storytelling. The Fool, shown as usual with a dog, leads Kaplan to a tale of a warrior who cut off a dog's head only to have the head save him from a poisonous snake. Another dog, in the card of the Moon, brings out a legend of a village terrorized by supernatural cats.

Different decks enter into their respective cultures at different levels. Not all Tarot designers will want to be as rigorous as the creators of the Native American Tarot. There are some people who find the Native American too sociological. Two decks in this section present Rom (Gypsy) images and ideas. Both come from members of the Romany people. In the Zigeuner Tarot the Rom elements become a part of Walter Wegmuller's highly personal style. Tarot Tzigane, however, seeks to create a genuine expression of the Romany vision. Its designer, Tchalaï, writes that she created this deck as an alternative to suggestions that she write a 'definitive' book on the history of her people.

Xultun Maya Tarot

When the Xultan Tarot first appeared, in 1976, it seemed to many people a strange idea. What did the Tarot, with its links to Kabbalah, have to do with the mythology and imagery of a people who flourished in Central America over a thousand years ago? Following the Mayan style the cards were vivid and mysterious (though this comes partly because most people will not understand the iconography). But they are not Tarot. Or so people thought.

Since Peter Balin first published his deck, attitudes have changed. Cultural Tarots have become a recognized branch of the tradition. If anything, we now might criticize Balin for not adhering rigorously enough to authentic Mayan beliefs. When he gives us a creation myth he says that it goes 'something like this'. He draws heavily on the essentially modern teachings of Carlos Castaneda's Don Juan books, leaving us uncertain at times where a particular doctrine originates. For example, Balin arranges the Major Arcana in four rows of five cards, with the Magician as well as the Fool set aside. This links the twenty cards to the twenty days of the Mayan month. Each row further joins with a stage in the development of a sorceror according to Don Juan. The Fool and the Magician can symbolize Castaneda and Don Juan, or any apprentice and master.

Balin's book, *The Flight of the Feathered Serpent*, tells us a great deal about the Mayans. We learn of their creation myths, their social structures and games, and the legend of Feathered Serpent, called by the Mayans Gukumatz, and more familiar to us by the Aztec name Quetzalcoatl. These ideas all inform the cards. Card 20, Judgement in most decks, becomes changed to Venus so that the final row of five cards will form a cosmological sequence ending in the Earth.

The Mayans developed the calendar as an

esoteric system, with each day having its own significance. The Xultan Tarot includes glyphs for each of the days at the bottom of the trump cards.

Mayan art is elaborate and detailed. Individual cards cannot create a full sense of this style. To go further, Balin has come up with the unusual idea of forming the entire Major Arcana into a tapestry, with each card like a piece in a jigsaw puzzle. We cannot reproduce the whole sequence, but we can get a glimpse of it in a few cards.

For the Minor cards Balin has devised a list of twenty-two correspondences for each suit, including season, direction, sexuality, orchestra, humours, and so on. The individual cards are given names based on the Golden Dawn designations. The four Sevens are titled Lord of Valor (Staffs), Warrior of Futility (Swords), Lady of Debauch (Cups), Servant

of Failure (Jades). This links each suit to a court card, for these also are Lord, Lady, Warrior, Servant.

The Minor cards themselves are simpler, but still vivid representations of Mayan imagery.

Native American Tarot

The Xultan Tarot helped open the way to cultural Tarots. The Native American Tarot, designed by Magda Gonzalez and painted by J. A. Gonzalez, shows how the cards can truly illuminate a specific culture. The cards feature aspects from the many different nations of North America. In the Five of Pipes (Wands) the picture adapts the design of the Rider pack – five boys clashing sticks –

to depict an Iroquois game which later became lacrosse. The traditional (Golden Dawn) designation for the Six of Wands, 'Victory', becomes Crazy Horse's victory over Custer.

While some cards, such as Strength, emphasize traditional Tarot images, and others, such as Corn Maiden (High Priestess), adapt the cards' inner qualities to a new

VICTORY

COUNTING COUP

STRENGTH

CORN MAIDEN

POLYGAMY

THE SLED

form, others tend to emphasize history and social customs. The Nine of Blades becomes the opportunity to delineate customs of polygamy, along with the information that few tribes practised it. The Chariot changes to the Sled, an image of the Inuit people of the far north.

The dedication of these cards to Native American culture has led some people, especially outside the United States, to see them as a curiousity, or even an annoyance. But the deck does not wholly abandon the Tarot's traditional meanings or purposes. In the best of the images, the cards give a new dimension of genuine practises while keeping the fundamental symbols.

MEDICINE WOMAN

SHAMAN

THE STARS

THE WORLD

Medicine Woman adapts the idea of the Empress to the concrete reality of healers. The Shaman does the same with the Hierophant idea. Together, the two cards also correct certain mistaken ideas people have had about Native American traditions, such as that healers were always medicine *men*, or that the healer and the holy person were the same. With such cards as The Stars and The World we enter the powerful scenes of Native American mythologies.

A number of new Tarots have changed some of the suit designations or the titles of the court cards. The Native American deck goes further than most, adapting all the names. The Suits are Blades (Swords), Pipes (Wands), Vessels (Cups), and Shields

MATRIARCH OF PIPES

CHIEF OF BLADES

(Pentacles). The court cards are Matriarch, Chief, Warrior, Maiden. These say something about the social structure of Native Americans. At the same time they keep close to the designations of at least those modern decks which replace Page with Princess. As with many individual cards, the titles take an abstract idea and show how it took shape among particular peoples. By making the Matriarch the head of the suit, and not the Chief, the deck teaches us the power and importance of women in America before the conquest.

The deck develops a coherent idea in a detailed and consistent fashion. A great deal of its success comes from the art, with its detailed realism joined to a sense of mystery and spiritual awareness. Unlike many decks, the art stays at the same level in the Minor cards as in the Major.

WARRIOR OF SHIELDS

MAIDEN OF VESSELS

DEATH

THE WEAVER

PREGNANCY

GIVE-AWAY DANCE

MATRIARCH OF SHIELDS

The Medicine Woman Tarot

Published in 1987, this deck by Carol Bridges was possibly influenced by the Native American Tarot. It too depicts aspects of daily life and spiritual belief as experienced by various Native American nations. The four suits appear to represent people of different areas (I do not have the *Medicine Woman Inner Guidebook* which probably would make this clearer). Bowls seem to be Polynesian, presumably Hawaiian.

In comparison with the Gonzalez deck, Bridges does not seek to bring alive the reality of tribal life so much as to use that life as an example of human possibilities, an alternative to the culture we know today. In the sheet that comes with the cards she writes that her deck 'is based on woman's love and respect for Mother Earth and all beings'.

The statement brings out the other main theme in this Tarot, that of women's spirituality. The images mostly show women, though not exclusively. The Hermit becomes a woman Guide, the Hanged Man changes to a woman seeing a Vision. Other figures, however, such as the Magician and the Emperor, remain male, while in one of her most imaginative scenes the Star changes to the Grandfathers, which then pairs with the next card, the Grandmothers (Moon).

The suits each follow a particular character, showing her in different situations and then at different stages of her life in the court cards. This main character is a woman in three of the suits, while Bowls shows a heterosexual couple.

The court cards in this deck travel further from tradition than most others. As well as Apprentice and Exemplar they include Totem

and Lodge. These two go beyond the depiction of people, to spiritual connections to the animal world (Totems) and the development of rituals within a community (Lodges).

The style is line drawings, often quite simple, done with imagination and sincerity.

The deck's strength lies in its imagination, shown in such cards as Discernment. Unfortunately, a sentimentality in many of the cards takes away from the impact. We see this in the Disney-like Seeker, and the overly cute children in Balance.

The pictures present an unrealistic view of tribal life, nearly always gentle, with very little pain. In the Major Arcana, the harshest image is the Trickster (Devil). It shows poverty and suffering. And yet, the description says, 'Words can fool you . . . The cause of your apparent trouble is in a negative idea you hold to be true.' We do need positive images to build individual lives and a harmonious society. But if a Tarot deck sets itself such goals it also needs to recognize the realities of injustice, pain, and suffering.

Norse Tarot

My knowledge of this deck comes from a very early stage in its production, with only black and white xeroxes of the pictures, and a short section of the manuscript, available to me. Despite this, many of the qualities of the cards come through, showing a deck with strongly drawn figures and fine background detail. The pictures emphasize action, sometimes going beyond the borders of the cards, as in the Five and Seven of Wands. Others,

such as the Eight of Wands and the Eight of Swords, give us unusual angles.

The image of the warrior is very strong in these cards, including a number of female images, such as the Empress and Death.

While the Major cards appear to feature scenes and characters from Norse mythology, the suit cards depict daily life among the medieval Vikings.

Some cards, such as the Moon, show a portrait of a mythological figure. Many others,

the empress

death

the high priestess

strength

the moon

the high priest

the chariot

such as the High Priest and the Chariot, depict an event.

This gives the cards an emphasis on stories rather than symbolism. In the introductory chapter to the book the deck's creator compares the structure of the major Arcana to traditional tales and legends.

The figure of Odin dominates Norse myth, and so we see him in various of the cards. The Magician appears to be Odin, as does the male figure in the Lovers. The Hanged Man makes the clear connection with Odin's self-sacrifice to gain the Runes from Mimir's Well. We know this myth from poems about Odin. Though the poems do not describe the God as hanging upside down, we do read of him reaching down to snatch up the Runes. This is difficult to imagine if Odin is hanging upright.

The trumps display a Rune on each card. The order does not follow the descriptions in the Edda, nor any of the better known Runic alphabets. The text, when ready, will probably make clear the reasons for the choices.

Celtic Tarot

The Celtic Tarot comes from Ti Birchrose, who lives in the wonderfully named town of Steamboat Plaza, Colorado. Birchrose had made only thirteen copies of this at the time of writing, drawing each one by hand rather than printing them. This makes each deck unique, a quality Birchrose emphasizes by instructing how to colour the cards (pencils or inks, rather than watercolours), but not which colours. She also suggests that the user can add her or his own designs. The robes of the people appear without decoration so that each person can draw symbols and images directly on to the characters.

Birchrose has based her drawings on Celtic art, especially decorative motifs. The Ace of Pentacles shows entwined puppet-like fig-ures, while the Star is a stylized maze floating above a woman's hands. In the Moon we see an elaborate version of the Celtic three-pronged spiral. A simpler version appears on

the back of the card. The design comes from a glyph to ward off evil.

The artist's respect for individual choice carries through in her ordering of the cards. There are no numbers on the trumps, allowing each person to choose whichever sequence seems correct. Similarly, the tip of the Ace of Wands can represent a bud or a flame. Birchrose describes the choice as between Air or Fire. I would have thought that the bud would suggest Earth rather than Air; more important, however, the cards give the user a choice, a concept not found in very many decks.

The Basque Mythical Tarot

The Euskal Tarot Mitikoa follows the traditional Tarot forms more closely than some of the other cultural Tarots we have been looking at. At the same time, its mountainous settings, its use of special symbols and imagery, and its simple style give it a sense of a glimpse into an ancient culture.

In each of these cards we find the traditional design in a mountainous rural community. Notice the wheel on the Fool's arm and the Magician's throat. Notice also that the Emperor and the Fool carry the same staff.

Such points can lead to various speculations and fantasies, such as a fairy-tale of a king and his lost son who becomes a magician.

The pictures are crude, with simple cartoon figures. The faces all appear looking out, even when the person stands sideways, as if the artist could not draw profiles. For myself, the naiveté works, increasing the charm of the deck.

A number of the cards show a flair for the fantastic. The Chariot radiates light. A kind of worm with two horse's heads pulls it,

while a face stares out from the front of it (compare the Chariot of Dali). The Wheel of Fortune depicts a Hercules-like figure lifting a huge phallic stone from a hole in the ground. A wheel adorns the stone and when we look closer we see, around the wheel, the tra-

ditional sphinx and ape, now joined by a fish. Death appears as a flaming tree, while behind the harvest of heads we see a group of pillars with the disc motifs found throughout the deck.

Fantasy emerges in the suit emblems as well. The Wands form a variant of the Fool/Emperor staff; the Ace is more elaborate, however, showing a Cyclops trying to uproot a tree with branches like snakes. On

the Ace of coins we see a mandala image, with faces on the first layer of petals.

The court cards show the same settings in each suit. The Pages – apparently young girls – all stand before caves, the Knights ride

before criss-crossed faces, the Queens sit in front of stone circles, while the kings, wear-

ing esoteric decorations, sit or stand by rock thrones.

Zigeuner Tarot

The Zigeuner Tarot was painted by Walter Wegmuller, the same artist who later created the Neuzeit Tarot. Somewhat simpler than the later deck, these cards show the same melting forms, distorted people, and extravagant imagery. It is interesting that the Moon, which often symbolizes wildness and strange fantasies, appears as the most ordered of the cards.

Zigeuner means Romany, or Gypsy, and Wegmuller, a Rom himself according to the pamphlet, has brought in ideas and images from Romany culture, though more as an influence than a systematic presentation. The Chariot is pulled by a goat and a chicken, animals common in a Romany camp. For the Moon the pamphlet describes the two dogs as originally 'the wild wolves of the Eastern

plain through which our ancestors journeyed'. The Knight of Staves shows the concern for horses in the culture, while the Hanged Man and the Page of Staves emphasize music. The Hanged Man is playing the violin with his foot, while the Page holds a sitar, reflecting

the people's origins in India.

A salesman, street artist, story-teller, and diviner, Wegmuller worked for a time with Sergius Golowin, a collector of Gypsy legends and traditions. The booklet for the cards apparently contains information from

THE EMPEROR
L'EMPEREUR

THE HIEROPHANT
LE PAPE

THE WHEEL OF FORTUNE
LA ROUE DE FORTUNE

THE TOWER
LA MAISON DIEU

Golowin's book *Die Welt des Tarot*, about Wegmuller and his cards. The two men suggest an interesting link of the Tarot's Kabbalist tradition with India and other Asian influences. They point out that the Khazars, a people from Siberia, converted to Judaism in the seventh century and remained a Jewish nation for some three hundred years. Now, most historians maintain that the Romany did not bring the Tarot to Europe but only encountered it when they came to Spain from North Africa. Nevertheless, we know of ancient card games in India. And the Khazars have received little or no attention in the formation of Jewish and therefore Kabbalist beliefs. The major cards follow the modern tradition of a Hebrew letter on each card.

The trumps also show rows of symbols on either side of the card and a kind of thought balloon above the central figure's head. Sometimes this balloon is blank, as in the Emperor, at other times it contains objects, such as the books above the Hierophant. This last is a nice touch, showing how the teacher conveys both oral and written knowledge to his disciples.

Many cards have subtle images calling for a closer look. The Wheel of Fortune rises from a boat, a common idea, but here the boat consists of two swan necks and heads, with the backs of the heads human faces. The Tower appears made of bricks, but when we look again we notice that each brick displays an image of modern life. The booklet tells us that if we invert the card we will see the people dancing to celebrate the coming of spring.

Tarot Tzigane

Much more than the German Zigeuner, this French deck, by journalist and writer Tchalaï, presents a rigorous depiction of Rom images and ideas. As well as the cards, the booklet celebrates the Romany people, beginning with poems and then a passionate account of Rom achievements in the face of bigotry. Two million Roms died in Nazi death camps, a vital fact about the Holocaust unknown to most people.

Tchalaï tells us that she created her deck as an alternative to an academic book on Rom history. The Rom peoples, she says, possess 'Tarots' which descend directly from 'Chaturanga' cards painted on round pieces of leather or mother-of-pearl by their ancestors, the 'Rajput Princes'. Tchalaï considers her deck free of 'pollution' by centuries of 'mistakes'. We might describe this assertion as over-reaching or inflated. It is, in fact, no different from the claims made by many Tarot designers, from esoteric to matriarchal, all of them insisting that this work has restored the true and correct Tarot.

Though the cards reflect Romany lives, they are not simply historical or sociological.

Some do show daily experience.

Others, however, give us symbolic or mythological images.

The wonderfully drawn Lotchilokos is an example of 'disruptive spirits with whom you must settle your accounts'. At the same time,

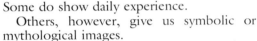

the tangled serpents symbolize wisdom, while the image of the gaping mouth recalls Tibetan demons. We learn that Lotchilokos are 'invincible and tormenting' in the dark, but can be forced to give presents when dragged into the light.

Aggarti signifies a more esoteric level of belief. Seven stars (possibly for the Pleiades, though the text does not say so) and the aurora borealis appear over a Horus-like eye of revelation set into the Earth. The Aggarti tradition describes a kind of astral travelling to a pyramid library with first 4000 sages, then 400, then 40, then 10, until the seeker finally reaches the pinnacle to discover 'a garden as limitless as the cosmos, the dwelling

of the THAGAR LUMEAKI, the very real King of the World.'

We are dealing with a vivid occult tradition, but also with myth that is alive and powerful. The deck develops the Rom account of their history, a descent from the Rajput Princes of India, who lost their kingdom and became dispersed in different bands. In The Battle of Terain we see one of these princes fighting an Arab warrior. But the deck also embraces the Rom belief that they descended from the stars, literally from space, and after their wanderings on Earth will return to the heavens. The cards and the descriptions treat this idea both literally and symbolically.

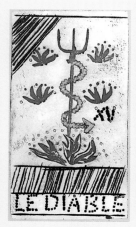

The Devil
Tarot de Louttre

Ace of Wands
Tarot de Louttre

The Emperor
Omaha Old Market

Force
Omaha Old Market

The Moon
Dali Universal Tarot

The World
Dali Universal Tarot

The World
I Tarocchi di Picini

The Moon
I Tarocchi di Picini

The Empress
I Tarocchi di Picini

The Sun
Tarocco Storico

Force
Tarocco Storico

The Emperor
Tarocco Storico

The Devil
(*far left*)
Omaggio a Erté

Death
(*middle*)
Omaggio a Erté

The Lovers
(*left*)
Omaggio a Erté

Wheel of Fortune
Collection Tarot

Queen of Batons
Collection Tarot

The Devil
Animal Tarot

King of Cups
Animal Tarot

The Angel
Fantastic Shoe Tarot

The Emperor
Divinatory Flower Tarot

Fortune
Divinatory Flower Tarot

The High Priestess
(*right*)
Smokers Tarot

The Hanged Man
(*far right*)
Smokers Tarot

The Tower
Tobacco Tarot

The Moon
Tobacco Tarot

The Empress
Musical Tarot

The Sun
Musical Tarot

The Lovers
Divinatory Hands Tarot

The Devil
Sardinia Tarot

The Sun
Sardinia Tarot

The Fool
Haindl Tarot

Ace of Cups
Haindl Tarot

The Sun God and the Pope from the Tarot
Garden of Niki de St Phalle

A view of the Tower, from the Tarot Garden of
Niki de St Phalle

Knave of Cups
Tarot Maddonni

Queen of Money
Tarot Maddonni

The Magician
Prager Tarot

Ace of Wands
Prager Tarot

Ace of Swords
Prager Tarot

Two of Coins
Prager Tarot

The Tower
Neuzeit Tarot

Judgement
Neuzeit Tarot

Strength
Neuzeit Tarot

The Lovers
Neuzeit Tarot

Judgement
(*right*)
Tarot of the Witches

Queen of Batons
(*far right*)
Tarot of the Witches

The Fool
Prediction Tarot

The Chariot
Prediction Tarot

The Emperor
Prediction Tarot

King of Coins
Prediction Tarot

King of Rods
Hanson-Roberts Tarot

The World
Hanson-Roberts Tarot

Ace of Cups
Hanson-Roberts Tarot

The Sun
Hanson-Roberts Tarot

The World
Sacred Rose Tarot

The Fool
Sacred Rose Tarot

Seven of Wands
Sacred Rose Tarot

Five of Wands
Sacred Rose Tarot

The High Priestess
(*far left*)
Solleone Tarot

THE HIGH PRIESTESS

Queen of Swords

Queen of Swords
(*middle*)
Solleone Tarot

Ace of Wands

Ace of Wands
(*left*)
Solleone Tarot

Birds and Fish
Future Solleone Tarot

The Madman
Future Solleone Tarot

Death
Future Solleone Tarot

Water
Future Solleone Tarot

Eight of Swords
Tarot of the Cat People

The High Priestess
Tarot of the Cat People

The Lovers
Tarot of the Cat People

Ace of Swords
Tarot of the Cat People

The Lovers
(*right*)
Mythic Tarot

The Tower
(*middle*)
Dante Tarot

The Lovers
(*far right*)
Minotarot

XXI PRIESTESS

The Priestess
Merlin Tarot

III STAR

The Star
Merlin Tarot

The Star
Xultan Maya Tarot

Death
Xultan Maya Tarot

THE WORLD

CHIEF OF BLADES

Exemplar of Bowls

The World
(*far left*)
Native American Tarot

Chief of Blades
(*middle*)
Native American Tarot

Exemplar of Bowls
(*left*)
Medicine Woman Tarot

The World
Basque Mythical Tarot

Knight of Coins
Basque Mythical Tarot

Wheel of Fortune
Basque Mythical Tarot

XXI   ANDRA MARI

EL MUNDO   ★   THE WORLD

ZALDIA   ★   CABALLO   ★   KNIGHT

URREAK   ★   OROS   ★   COINS

X   ITZULARRI

LA RUEDA DE LA FORTUNA   ★   WHEEL OF FORTUNE

THE MAGICIAN   LE BATELEUR

RITTER-STAB
KNIGHT OF WANDS   CAVALIER DES BÂTONS

THE HIEROPHANT   LE PAPE

THE TOWER   LA MAISON DIEU

The Magician
Zigeuner Tarot

Knight of Wands
Zigeuner Tarot

The Hierophant
Zigeuner Tarot

The Tower
Zigeuner Tarot

The Chariot
(*right*)
Tarot Tzigane

Mother of Coins
(*middle*)
Tarot Tzigane

Father of Staves
(*far right*)
Tarot Tzigane

The Phoenix
Secret Dakini Oracle

The Fool
Secret Dakini Oracle

The Holocaust
Secret Dakini Oracle

19 PHOENIX

0 JOKER

16 HOLOCAUST

High Priestess
Kashmir Tarot

Judgement
Kashmir Tarot

The Devil
Kashmir Tarot

Six of Swords
Ukiyoe Tarot

Nine of Cups
Ukiyoe Tarot

The Wheel of Fortune
Tarot of Transition

Queen of Staves
Tarot of Transition

The Labourer
(*far left*)
Egipcios Kier Tarot

Justice
(*middle*)
Egipcios Kier Tarot

High Priestess
(*left*)
Egipcios Kier Tarot

VII

Chariot

4

Wands

The Chariot
(*far left*)
Motherpeace Tarot

Four of Wands
(*left*)
Motherpeace Tarot

Grâce   Grazia
Grazie   Gracia
Grace

Trois des Coupes   Tre di Coppe
Three of Cups
Drei-Kelche   Tres de Copas

6

Les Amoureux   Gli Amanti
The Lovers
Die Liebenden   Los Enamorados

Galahad

Prince des Coupes   Principe di Coppe
Prince of Cups
Prinz der Kelche   Principe de Copas

Three of Cups
Barbara Walker Tarot

The Lovers
Barbara Walker Tarot

Prince of Cups
Barbara Walker Tarot

Anger

Four of Cups

Ace of Worlds

Illumination

Ace of Wands

Four of Cups
(*far left*)
Voyager Tarot

Ace of Worlds
(*middle*)
Voyager Tarot

Ace of Wands
(*left*)
Voyager Tarot

URSPRUNG
ORIGINE
ORIGIN
33

TEILEN
PARTAGER
SHARING
20

Origin
(*far left*)
Philosopher's Stone

Sharing
(*left*)
Philosopher's Stone

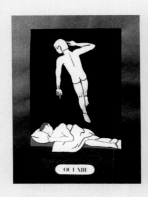

OUT XIII

TENSION I

DRAGON II

Out
(*far left*)
David Findlay

Tension
(*middle*)
David Findlay

Dragon
(*left*)
David Findlay

Squares
Isis Tarot

Jack of Clubs
Kirwan Cards

Three of Hearts
Kirwan Cards

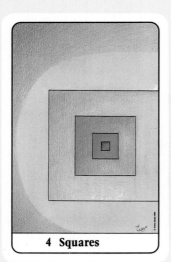

4 Squares

The Fool
(*right*)
Golden Dawn Tarot

The Emperor
(*middle*)
Golden Dawn Tarot

Princess of Cups
(*far right*)
Golden Dawn Tarot

0 THE FOOL

4 THE EMPEROR

PRINCESS OF CUPS

The Tree of Life
(*right*)
Tree of Life Tarot

The Lovers,
(*middle*)
Tree of Life Tarot

The Moon
(*far right*)
Tree of Life Tarot

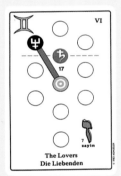

עץ ה חיים
Âtz ha Chaim

THE TREE OF LIFE — DER BAUM DES LEBENS

The Lovers
Die Liebenden

The Moon
Der Mond

The High Priestess
Magickal Tarot

The Universe
Magickal Tarot

Lust For Life
Magickal Tarot

The High Priestess

The Universe

Lust For Life

Six of Cups
Norse Tarot

Five of Disks
Norse Tarot

Two of Swords
Norse Tarot

The Tower
Norse Tarot

The Magician
Enoil Gavat Tarot

The Fool
Enoil Gavat Tarot

The Star
Enoil Gavat Tarot

The Moon
Enoil Gavat Tarot

The Star
(*far left*)
Stairs of Gold Tarot

The Emperor
(*middle*)
Stairs of Gold Tarot

Queen of Cups
(*left*)
Stairs of Gold Tarot

The Hermit
Mandala Astrological Tarot

The High Priest
Mandala Astrological Tarot

The Moon
Mandala Astrological Tarot

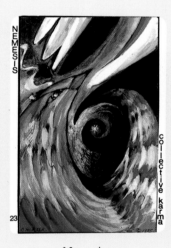

Venus
Astrotaro

Nemesis
Astrotaro

Lunar Nodes
Astrotaro

The High Priestess
(*right*)
Masonic Tarot

The Hermit
(*middle*)
Masonic Tarot

Ace of Wands
(*far right*)
Masonic Tarot

Star
El Gran Tarot Esoterica

The Emperor
El Gran Tarot Esoterica

The High Priestess
El Gran Tarot Esoterica

Queen of Swords
El Gran Tarot Esoterica

Temperance
Gareth Knight Tarot

Strength
Gareth Knight Tarot

The Emperor
Gareth Knight Tarot

Ace of Disks
Gareth Knight Tarot

The Triple Magus
(*far left*)
Elksinger's Perfected Tarot

Truth
(*left*)
Elksinger's Perfected Tarot

O Geape Vimanaki, the next to last trump, shows a kind of lingam and yoni figure, the union of male and female. However, it also shows a spaceship, the Vimana, which brought the Romani to Earth and will one day return them. The final trump, Tataghi (Heart of Fire) makes clear the symbolic meaning of this journey, for it describes 'the return of the Rom to his origin – cosmic and divine'.

We can describe this story as the basic myth of all Tarots, with the Fool in ordinary decks as the lost wanderer, and the Major Arcana as the journey which ends with a 'return' to the cosmos. However, the link here to a specific cultural belief gives the story greater depth and conviction. It becomes something more than a symbol for psychological growth.

Tarot Tzigane consists of twenty-two Arcana, loosely corresponding to the trumps of ordinary decks, plus twelve cards similar to court cards and four similar to Aces. The people are Father, Mother, and Child. The other four are Tools. Tchalaï has chosen his four 'suits' to honour the main Romany branches, the Kalderash of Central Europe, the Manush of Northern Italy, the Gypsies of Ireland, and the Gitanos of Andalusia (Spain). The Tools link the cards to the traditional Tarot suits. They are Kalderash – swords, knives, scalpels; Manush – coins; Gypsies – pots, hoods, containers; and Gitanos – wooden stick, musical instrument. (The Zigeuner Tarot also connects Staves to instruments.)

Graphist Monique Arnold, a non-Tzigane, worked closely with Tchalaï to create a deck that would rework traditional Rom images and style. The black and white figures shine

against a background either red, blue, gold, or green, colours suggesting the four elements.

People used to traditional occult or divinatory Tarots may pass by the Tzigane Tarot. They make a mistake if they do. Its evocation of a mythology, an esoteric system, and a way of life deserves our attention.

Ravenswood Eastern Tarot

The two Rom Tarots both refer to the origins of the Romany in India. Dirk Dykstra's Eastern Tarot takes East Indian and Turkish imagery from the nineteenth century and applies it to the classic Pamela Smith designs of the Rider pack. The style of these black and white cards is simple, and in the Minor cards crude.

When he adds a cultural influence, such as the yogi ascetic on the Four of Swords or Eight of Cups, the additional content makes the cards interesting. Otherwise, they simplify Smith without contributing anything new. The court cards have a certain charm, for they depict the Indian nobility. The

 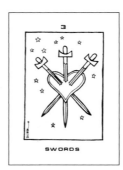  

knights all ride animals suited to their elements.

For the Major cards Dykstra has created more elaborate and more original designs. Cards such as the Devil and Judgement adapt the standard images to Indian mythology (oddly, the text for Judgement suggests that Siva is a Goddess).

The deck attempts to develop a precise language of symbols. The instructions tell us that stars represent spiritual forces, foliage represents potential for growth, flowers are celebration, water cleansing, fire invigorating, clouds open and honest. We learn that others exist as well. Most Tarot decks will invest particular images with particular meanings, but usually not so extensively. Unfortunately, the limited drawing style does not develop this attempt at a full Tarot iconography.

The black and white cards come with colouring instructions, but also with the suggestion that we follow our own feelings. As mentioned above, this departs from previous occult ideas where each colour carried a vibratory power independent of individual preferences.

HIGH PRIESTESS

WHEEL OF FORTUNE

THE DEVIL

JUDGMENT

Secret Dakini Oracle

Nik Douglas is a scholar of Sanskrit, and Tibetan culture. He has worked with Penny Slinger, a collage artist, to create a set of cards based on sixty-four carvings of dancing figures known as 'Dakinis', representations of the 'female principle' of intuitive wisdom. Though female, this energy resides within each person, sometimes creative, sometimes destructive, but necessary for existence. (Douglas does not explain what makes the energy female if it resides within everyone.) In the book that comes with the cards, Douglas tells us that Dakini means the same as Shakti, a Hindu term better known in the West. The Dakinis, he goes on to say, guard the 'deeper mysteries of the Self'. He compares them as well to Gnosis, 'the female principle of transforming Wisdom', and tells us that they act on the Navel or Solar Plexus (his capitals) to transform the self, for 'all psychological components of personality

exist as Energies in the Navel Center'. Douglas quotes the Tibetan sage Naropa about using meditation to merge with the Dakinis. He and Slinger have created the cards for people to use the same technique. They describe their purposes as divination, meditation, and 'personality transformation'.

Sixty-four statues would seem to relate more to the *I Ching*, with its sixty-four hexagrams, than the Tarot. However, as a visual medium, without a fixed text, the Tarot opens itself to fusion with other visual forms. Douglas does not claim that the Tarot originated with the Dakinis. He simply suggests a value in bringing the two together.

The Secret Dakini Oracle contains sixty-five cards: twenty-two based closely on the Major Arcana, forty supposedly based on the four elements, and three Time cards, past, present, and future. The forty 'suit' cards in fact bear individual titles, like trumps, and

53 TREE SPIRIT / YAKSHI

60 TAKING UP ARMS

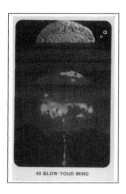

40 BLOW YOUR MIND

25 THREE-FOLD RIDDLE

connect only thematically to Fire, Water, etc. They range from directly mystical images, such as 53, Tree Spirit, to plays on language, like 60, Taking Up Arms, to psychobabble clichés, such as 40, Blow Your Mind. One card, 25, Three-fold Riddle, displays an insensitivity to the sometimes hard and oppressive realities of an alien culture. Showing the hideous 'veils' worn by women in Afghanistan, the card supposedly represents the 'unrevealed aspect of a triad of forces'. We are told that they confuse us with 'their mysterious dance of illusion'. This is romanticism of the worst sort.

The major cards include traditional Tibetan images, such as 19, Pheonix, or 10, Wheel of Great Time. Other cards follow the Tarot more exactly.

19 PHOENIX

10 WHEEL OF GREAT TIME

1 MERCURY

2 ISIS / THE HIGH PRIESTESS

A number of cards (in the elements as well as the trumps) use contemporary scenes or objects.

At their best, Penny Slinger's cards give us striking images taken from science as well as myth. Unfortunately, Nik Douglas's text tends to vague statements meant as cosmic wisdom.

0 JOKER

16 HOLOCAUST

4 HOT SEAT

15 ALLY

21 EARTH BOUND

Kashmir Tarot

In 1982, on the full Moon of the Buddha's birthday, the Dutch artist Nicolaas van Beek conceived the idea of creating a set of carvings from the twenty-two Tarot trumps. An esotericist who had received initiation into Tibetan Buddhism, he wanted to incorporate Tibetan ideas into the Tarot tradition. He was in India at the time, and decided to travel to Kashmir, an area famous for its wood-carvers. Working with carver Abdul Salama, he completed a prototype set of carvings on another full Moon, the birthday of Shiva.

Twenty-two sets of these carvings exist, making the original Kashmor Tarot one of the world's rarest contemporary decks. Van Beek then decided to create a set of actual cards which he could print for a wider public. At the same time, he wanted to give this printed version the same care – and respect – given to the carvings. Instead of using stand-ard four-colour printing, the pictures were silk-screened on to bristol cardboard, allow-ing exact colour reproduction and ink texture. The process took a year, with van Beek and Dik Al, his printer, repeating the printing sequence some one hundred thousand times. Luckily for the two men, they saw this not simply as labour (even a labour of love) but a spiritual training, a way of merging with the cards.

The Kashmir Tarot stays very close to tra-ditional Tarot images, for van Beek was seek-ing a genuine synthesis, rather than using the Tarot as an excuse for presenting classic Tibetan symbols and theology. He does not suggest that Tarot originally comes from Tibet. On the contrary, he respects Tarot as a Western system, and therefore a base to bring together two mystical experiences, East and West. On the card of the Magician, we see a figure wearing a Tibetan head-dress, but otherwise with the usual wand and emblems of the four suits. An Egyptian God (Horus or Ra-Harakhte) stands before him, a further blending of traditions. The High Priestess sits before the Tibetan mountains, but holds the Tora scroll in her lap.

A number of cards utilize the magnificent setting of the Himalayas. Death sets Egyptian imagery in a mountain ravine. Hands emerge from the mandala, one holding a sword, the other the barest suggestion of a cup. In Judgement a Christian angel awakens three initiates. Their bodies form the word 'Lux', that is, light.

From the beginning of his painting, van Beek recognized that the medium offered more opportunity for subtle design than the

circles, triangles, squares, and other shapes represent both fundamental energy and abstract ideas. The traditional Tarot relies on a recurrent triangular motif, seen in such cards as the Hierophant and his two disciples, or the Chariot and his two horses or sphinxes. The Kashmir Tarot develops this symbolism as well as making it explicit.

In the card of the Lovers we see a scene similar to Waite or Crowley, a man and woman with a mountain behind them and an angel above. We also see a series of circles, including the suggestion of an overall circle containing the entire scene. The circles symbolize the development of unity through love. The first circles, around the two people's heads, remain isolated from each other. The second level touches, while the third circles interlock. The interlocking creates a yoni, a female genital symbol, while the line from the angel to the mountain suggests the phallic lingam.

original carvings. As well as depicting delicate scenes he has organized the energy appropriate to each card through lines and circles of light. Compare the graceful spirals on Judgement to the sharp triangles of the Devil, in which the wings and the positions of the people seem to emerge out of underlying patterns.

Geometry has long served as a primary symbol in occultism. By their pure form

Ukiyoe Tarot

The Ukiyoe style of art comes from the Edo period of Japan, beginning in the seventeenth century, when the Shoguns rules the country. As shown in this Tarot deck, the Ukiyoe style used delicate colour and fine detail to depict the lives of ordinary people.

Ukiyoe art, favoured by the middle class, focused on urban life, with particular attention for such people as actors, geishas, samurai, and so on. Quite early it became connected to Kabuki theatre, which began at about the same time.

Stuart Kaplan has admired Ukiyoe art for many years. In 1982 he realized a long-term

THE MAGICIAN

THE LOVERS

PAGE OF PENTACLES

THE FOOL

THE WHEEL OF FORTUNE

STRENGTH

ambition when he published this deck, painted under his supervision by Koji Foruta.

The cards follow traditional Tarot patterns. The Fool shows a tramp with a dog, Strength a woman with a lion. The Wheel of Fortune even includes a snake going down the wheel and a fox – like the jackal on some Egyptian inspired versions of this card – going up. The animals could easily represent Typhon and Anubis, the Egyptian Gods of death and rebirth.

And yet, the cards are completely Japanese. The Wheel shows the Buddhist Wheel of Doctrine, while Kaplan's comments point out that serpents and foxes often figured in Japanese folk tales, where they took on human forms. The Fool depicts a famous story of a warrior named Tametomo, who beheaded his dog when the dog annoyed him by barking, only to have the dog's head

THE CHARIOT

DEATH

fly up into a tree and kill a snake.

The Chariot and Death show images more specifically Japanese. In Death we see Emma-

PAGE OF SWORDS

KING OF PENTACLES

hoo, the Japanese Buddhist God of Death, who wears the robes of a Chinese judge in order to examine the souls of the dead and determine how long each must stay in Hell before rebirth (compare the Egyptian Tarot of Transition). The Chariot gives us another hero tale, that of Raiko, who disguised himself as a monk in order to kill a demon. This subtly changes the card's meaning, for instead of indicating victory through will power, it demonstrates triumph through cunning and physical force.

The court cards mix social types with specific people. The Page of Swords depicts Hideyoshi, a peasant who gained great power, while the King of Pentacles is Yoshimitsu, the first shogun to live in splendour as a ruler. The pip cards show flowers, and on the Cups animals. The Six of Swords displays the famous cherry blossoms.

In this deck, Kaplan demonstrates his flair for story-telling. The Moon presents a traditional image, a crab and two dogs, with a pair of towers, one dark, one light.
Kaplan tells us first that the dogs may be protecting the temples and villages from supernatural creatures, for ghosts often

invaded temples. He then goes on to describe a village terrorized by supernatural cats who demanded the sacrifice of a virgin girl once a year. A warrior decided to defend them and learned in a dream that the cats feared a dog named Schippeitaro. After describing the rescue, Kaplan compares the former danger of the supernatural at night with the 'mysterious and sometimes fearful manifestations of the subsconscious'.

Two Egyptian Tarots

In the eighteenth century Antoine Court de Gebelin declared the Tarot to be the 'Book of Thoth', the legendary book of all wisdom composed by the Egyptian God of magic and handed down to his disciples. Despite the lack of historical evidence for this idea it has become a Tarot myth, with many decks and books still asserting that the Tarot originated in Egypt. Over the years various Tarot decks have used Egyptian imagery. The most famous of these is Aleister Crowley's Thoth Tarot, painted by Lady Frieda Harris. Most of these decks, however, have used the style of ancient Egyptian art without really taking

on the beliefs or myths as the Egyptians themselves knew them. The two decks shown here, the Tarot of Transition and the Egipcios Kier, give us a more authentic sense of Egyptian life and religion as they really were. The Tarot of Transition does this especially, for it shows the Gods and rulers. Further, it uses the Egyptian concept of judgement in the afterlife to present a new and coherent system for using the cards. The Egipicos Kier deck follows the traditional trump images more closely but transforms the Minor cards into a catalogue of Egyptian society and daily life.

Tarot of Transition

While keeping the official names of the trumps at the bottom of each card, the Tarot of Transition transforms the pictures into

twenty-two Gods and Goddesses, many of them little known to those who have not made a special study of the mythology. They

impress us first of all with their accuracy. While the Universe remains closer than most to conventional Tarot design, the Fool abandons the usual Egyptian Tarot picture of a walker menaced by a crocodile. It is interesting that Isis serves as the Empress rather than the High Priestess, while Ma'at, Goddess of divine order, appears as the Hermit rather than presiding over the Wheel of fortune. Beyond this sense of authenticity, the pictures are direct, but drawn with detail and precision.

The descriptions of the cards tell us little about the mythology for the particular deity. Though this seems to miss an opportunity, the pictures would still aid anyone who wanted to explore the stories and theology for themselves. This would involve finding a good account of Egyptian mythology and using it as a supplement to the booklet that comes with the cards. A person taking this initiative might find that the Tarot of Transition becomes a truly mythic Tarot, embodying the characters in bright vivid images.

Instead of describing the cards individually the deck constructs an essential story, that of the soul receiving judgement after death. This story then serves as a model, a myth, for Tarot consultation, so that instead of using ordinary spreads, with each card having a fortune-telling or psychological meaning, the deck instructs us to re-enact the soul's appearance before its judges.

The story takes the cards out of sequence. It begins conventionally with Bes, the Magus (1), and ends with Geb, the Universe (21),

and Hu-Tepa, the Fool (22). In between, however, the cards move around. Bes, 'a protective deity from the land of Punt', aids you in your request. Yumteph, the Hierophant, and Samaref, the High Priestess, then speak for you, while Hathor, the Lovers, takes you under 'their' (sic) protection. The story goes on, with various dangers and protections. It includes travelling across the underground Nile in the boat of the dead, Neshmet, the Chariot. Finally, Thoth, Justice, and Ma'at, the Hermit, determine the judgement and present their findings to Osiris, the Emperor, and Isis, the Empress. In the mythic terms of the story, if the judgement goes against you, Ammit, the Devil, will devour you. But if the judgement favours you, then Geb, the Universe, promises you delights, while Hu-Tepa, the Fool, helps you enjoy them.

The descriptions describe each card as

Favorable, Unfavorable, or Destiny. In readings the Destiny cards 'determine how the actual drama is going to be played'. To read the cards, the persons mixes the deck, then turns them over in rows of seven until the cards Å-Death, and Thoth-Justice appear. The reader then examines the influences, beginning with those closest to Å and Thoth.

The court cards consist of Pharoah, Queen, Charioteer, and Ushabti. The Ushabtis are helper spirits. Mythologically, they assist the person in her or his task in the Land of the Dead. Their inclusion gives the story a more personal quality, like the fairy tales in which animals help the hero or heroine accomplish some impossible assignment. In fact, all the court cards act as helpers, with the Ushabti the weakest. When the Pharoah and Queen appear together, the person can expect fulfilment of the promises shown in the trumps.

The four suits are Ankh, the key of life, Ded, the backbone of Osiris, Heset, the communion chalice (Christian communion possibly derives from the much earlier practise in the religion of Osiris), and Kheprera, the Sun, which appears as the sacred scarab.

In a reading, when the person has found the judgement with the trumps, she or he mixes the fifty-six Minor cards to create an 'amulet' which will help bring positive results. This approach to the cards, along with the general story for reading the Major Arcana, may strike some people as too close to fortune-telling or a superstitious belief that the cards control our lives. For others it may give them a new way of looking at their situations, as the acting out of mythic patterns.

Egipcios Kier

Even more than Tarot of Transition the Egipcios Kier deck marries the Tarot to ancient Egyptian culture and religion. We see cards of professions, such as Labourer, or Weaver, while other cards present social arrangements, such as Magnificence, for which the commentary tells us how nobles set up their households, how they managed servants and slaves, and so on.

23 ♀ The Laborer T 5

24 ♀ The Weaver U 6

32 ☿ Magnificence D 5

♌♂ Resurrection ˥ 20

Much of the information has to come from the descriptions rather than the pictures, making this one of the few decks which is truly incomplete without the instructions. In Magnificence we only see two people at table. In the card of Resurrection we find a striking mythological figure over a sarcophagus. The text not only explains the image, it also details for us the Egyptian theology of the soul, death, and afterlife. The cards originally came from a publisher in Argentina. The instructions for the American edition are by Stuart Kaplan, raising the possibility that most of the information comes from Kaplan's own research (and speculations). If so, he has done his work so well that the descriptions become an integral part of the deck's ability to immerse us in Egyptian life.

The style of drawing lacks some of the subtlety of line of Tarot of Transition. On the other hand, with all the Minor cards showing actual scenes, the Egipcios Kier provides far more information. Religion and myth are certainly present, but only as aspects of society. The pattern story of Tarot of Transition appears here as a single card, Examination, with Thoth and Ma-at judging a soul while Ammit waits below. Ma'at, or rather a worshipper of Ma'at, also appears on the trump Justice. In general, the Major cards show the human followers rather than the Gods themselves. For the High Priestess we see a priestess of Isis rather than Isis herself. One exception is the High Priest, Anubis.

The design of the trump cards follows previous Egyptian based Tarots. We see the

54 ♂ Examination Y 9

♄♑ Justice ˥˥ 8

☽♋ The Priestess ⊐ 2

☿♍ The High Priest ˥˥ 5

Fool as a young man with a crocodile. The Chariot is drawn by different coloured sphinxes, while the Wheel of Fortune has much of the symbolism familiar from standard esoteric decks. While it makes sense to use Egyptian images that are already in the tradition it can make the trump cards seem obvious, not as fresh as the original Minors.

The deck uses a detailed code of symbolism to give the cards an esoteric dimension. For the Major Arcana we see at the top of each card a hieroglyph, an alchemical sigil, and a letter from a magical alphabet found in *The Key of Solomon the King*, a grimoire translated by MacGregor Mathers, founder of the Golden Dawn. At the bottom of each card, along with the title and number, we find a planetary symbol, a zodiacal sign, and a Hebrew letter. The Minor cards contain at the top a Hebrew letter, a hieroglyph, and a letter from a magical alphabet. At the bottom are the card's number (there are no suits or court cards), a planetary symbol, a Roman letter, and a number corresponding to the magical letter above. The Hebrew letters on the Minor cards go in sequence but begin and end in the middle of the alphabet. The original Spanish edition of the cards may have worked all this symbolism into some coherent system. In the American edition Kaplan does virtually nothing with it. It is simply there, for people to use as they wish.

The Tarot of Transition, and especially the Egipcios Kier demonstrate the new rigour that has come into cultural Tarots. Where earlier decks borrowed Egyptian imagery for their own purposes, these two decks attempt, as much as possible, to give us a popular view of Egyptian beliefs and daily life as they really were.

CHAPTER 5
Women's Tarots

In its beginnings the modern women's movement identified itself with such classic political ideals as socialism and civil rights. At the same time, the small talk groups emphasized personal experience and co-operation as the basic method of liberation. Some time ago, many women began to look at religion from a feminist viewpoint. While this began with criticisms of male-dominated traditions, such as Christianity and Judaism, it quickly moved to an exploration of the possibilities for woman-centered spirituality. On the one side, this consists of developing ideas and practises directly from women's experience, through co-operation and experiment rather than theology and official hierarchies. On the other side, it involves recovering the thousands of years of Goddess worship in cultures all around the world. Our modern sense of history goes back only five thousand years, to the beginnings of patriarchal culture and religion. For many thousands of years before that, the Great Goddess 'of ten-thousand names' dominated humanity's sense of the sacred.

The return of the Goddess means the return of history – or 'herstory', as many women call the suppressed account of women's lives and religion. It also means creating a new knowledge of the sacred based on ancient beliefs and practises. For both purposes many women have begun to look to the Tarot as a vital tool. As a picture book the Tarot allows us to show things instead of just describing them. We can use it

to create images of Goddesses, and of alternative ways of life.

Because the Tarot lacks a definite origin and an official text or explanation people have felt free to put forth their own theories (usually declaring them as fact). Women have seized on this freedom to create a Tarot that is Pagan and matriarchal. Indeed, certain images have always pointed in this direction, such as the Papess, or the Empress, or the Star, or the World, the last card usually shown as a dancing woman. These have allowed some women to claim the Tarot as an underground holy book for Goddess-worshipping Witches forced to hide their doctrines from the Christian Church.

If we consider this idea far-fetched, or without evidence, it is no more so than many other suggestions. This does not mean we should not criticize specious claims. If a deck, such as Motherpeace, or Barbara Walker, takes herstory as a primary focus then we have the right to demand accuracy.

Women in the Goddess movement consciously see themselves as creating a new world. They reject not only past authorities, but the very concept of a doctrine which everyone must follow without deviance. They remember the millions of women burned as witches. In the Tarot this can lead to a Tarot lacking the weight of tradition. More positively, it brings freedom of re-imagination. While the decks shown here base themselves on Tarot structures and ideas they also take for themselves the freedom to start over, to make it new. The esoteric tradition often includes fixed symbols which particular cards must include. There is no such orthodoxy here. Some people may feel that this produces interesting pictures – but not Tarot. For myself, the best of these cards (by no means all of them) transform Tarot traditions through women's own experiences and visions.

The concern for co-operation rather than leadership has led to collective Tarots. The Daughters of the Moon contains work by eight artists, though the designer, Ffiona Morgan, designed all the cards. The New Amazon Tarot goes further. The women who conceived the deck developed the subjects but left the imagery entirely to the twenty-two artists.

The decks share various themes. Most show Goddesses for the trumps, and sometimes the Minor cards as well. They emphasize a life devoted to nature and peaceful community. In place of the prettiness most people think of as proper for images of women, they show women who are old, or big, or differently abled, women who are angry, or muscular, as well as women who are soft, or nurturing.

While some of these decks contain what

Billie Potts calls 'token men', they clearly emphasize women's experience, and especially women's experience apart from men. This will no doubt trouble some people, who will accuse these decks of simply reversing prejudice. But most women's Tarot decks have made a decision not to concern themselves with men. Patriarchal religion has always claimed to speak for women as well as men (and indeed for the whole universe), while giving women an inferior role. By and large, women's Tarots do not try to speak for men or give men particular roles. They describe the experiences of women.

The great danger in these decks is a soft nostalgia for an imagined lost paradise of Mother-love. Alongside this comes the belief that pain and violence are imposed on us by the distortions of patriarchy. And yet, if we can fault the decks (and not all of them) for ignoring the harsh sufferings of life, we should not ignore their imagination, or the value of their historical knowledge, or their ambition. For while esoteric decks promise a transformation of the self, women's Tarots seek a transformation of culture. Through images we create the world. Through images we can remake it.

Motherpeace

The Motherpeace Tarot, designed by Vicki Noble and drawn by Karen Vogel, has created a sensation. 'The Round Deck', as some people call it (though other, lesser known women's decks are also round) has expanded many people's ideas of what Tarot can be, as well as bringing people to a knowledge of ancient Goddesses and their implications for our contemporary world. Vicki Noble calls her book on the deck, *Motherpeace: A Way to the Goddess through Myth, Art, and Tarot.*

Like other women's Tarots, the deck seeks nothing less than to transform the world through images. As well as signifying the Moon and the female roundness of the Mother Goddess, the round shape symbolizes

a different approach to life, one marked by wholeness and community rather than the sharp corners of patriarchal thinking. For Noble and others the rectangular shape implies rigid structures, fixed ideas, and a hierarchy of leaders and followers. In readings, traditional decks often have upright and reversed meanings, with an implication of right and wrong. Round cards allow more shades of meaning, including the idea of waxing and waning influences. Curiously, though Noble tells how to read this way, she then gives standard upright and reversed interpretations for each card.

The Motherpeace deck develops two strategies for the transformation it seeks. On the one hand, it provides historical infor-

mation, images of ancient Goddesses, evidences of woman-centered religion in prehistoric times, facts about conquest by patriarchal invaders, speculations about the spread of Goddess religion to the Americas, and so on. Now, much of this information exists elsewhere, in greater detail. But Motherpeace presents it as *pictures*, and further, as Tarot cards, which people will want to study so that they can use them in readings. Further still, since people do use cards and not simply study them, the information, and the beliefs

behind it, can slowly move through people's lives, changing them, and through them the world. The deck's creators clearly hope for such an effect.

For such a purpose the book becomes as important as the pictures. The card of the Magician shows a shaman performing a ritual. Karen Vogel's picture is not historical; she has built it out of influences from different cultures. However, it gives Vicki Noble's text an opportunity to describe the female origins of spirituality, with the theory that this later

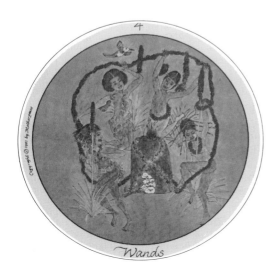

split into male shamanism and female fertility. The information is theoretical, but Noble backs it with descriptions of early cave paintings of pregnant women with animal heads, and surrounded by animals. The picture needs the text to complete it.

The Chariot gives us a more historical image, that of the Greek Goddess Athena, and above her the Egyptian Goddess of the Night Sky, Nut. Citing Robert Graves among others, Noble links both Goddesses to the Libyan Neith. She also uses Athena to introduce the subject of Amazons.

The other strategy is to provide images of alternative ways of life, where women are honoured, people truly admire peace rather than conquest, work gets done through co-operation rather than coercion, and so on. Some of the images show celebrations of life, such as the Four of Wands. This picture is meant as an archaic ritual for a girl's first menstruation.

The Star shows a woman immersed in water (compare it to the traditional image of a woman pouring water). It suggests various healing and purification ceremonies. In her commentary, Vicki Noble cites a cleansing ritual created by Z. Budapest for victims of rape. Noble also quotes Navajo and Tibetan prayers for restoration. Vogel's image is simple and serene.

Reactions to the art in Motherpeace have been mixed; some see it as exciting, even inspirational, others consider it amateurish and crude. For myself, I find the pictures themselves mixed. While some, such as the Priestess of Wands, or the Crone, show figures with weight and expressiveness, others, like the Ace of Cups, have very little development.

A deck that sets itself such high goals demands judgement by high standards. To my mind, there are many problems with Motherpeace. For one thing, Noble's book is sometimes sloppy on points of fact regarding the Tarot. She writes, 'Traditionally the Magician represented Aries', whereas most decks assign the card to Mercury. There are similar mistakes with other astrological correspondences. Noble tells us, 'One of the earliest Wheels of Fortune was inscribed with the words: The Tarot speaks the law of Hathor.' This sentence, a 'translation' of the anagrammatic 'Rota Taro Orat Tora Ator', goes back no further than the end of last century. These points may seem trivial, but if a deck works so much through historical evidence, we need to trust the accuracy of its information.

Motherpeace shows an ambivalent attitude to men. While clearly addressing itself primarily to women it now and then includes either a token male or a picture of patriarchy as the source of the world's troubles. The court cards are Priestess, Shaman, Daughter, and Son. The Shamans are one male and three female. As a friend of mine has pointed out, this implies a lack of adult roles for men.

More serious than either of these points is the question of how well the deck reflects reality. In its desire to show us a different way, Motherpeace romanticizes the ancient world, presenting it as a Golden Age of joy and harmony, as if the pain and suffering of our own experience come only through the imposition of patriarchy. Writing about the card of Death, Vicki Noble comments, 'When Death comes too soon, as it does so often in the world today. . .'. In physical terms this is a very strange assertion. For the first time in human history, the great mass of people has the chance to live to old age. If we think of it as a spiritual idea, with 'too soon' meaning before a person finds fulfilment, why should we assume that people found completeness in their lives more easily in other times and places? Noble makes the important point that our culture denies death in everyday life while using it as a constant threat through nuclear and other weapons. If we overcome our own fear of death, she says, we can also overcome our hopelessness about the arms race and so do something to end it. To do this, however, we need to recognize that our fear of dying, like so many other things that trouble us, goes down to very deep levels. If the Tarot helps us to confront our own reality while showing us another possibility, then it can lead to genuine transformation. To do this it needs to root out any tendency to easy solutions or romantic distortion. Alongside despair the greatest enemy of change is sentimentality.

Despite these problems, Motherpeace is an important deck, in its influence as well as its commitment. Its images and ideas can expand our awareness, not just of Tarot, but of women and spirituality.

Barbara Walker Tarot

Most books about a particular deck are written to accompany the cards. The Barbara Walker Tarot comes from illustrations Walker created for her book *The Secrets of the Tarot*. Walker describes herself as a researcher. Her book details a vast amount of information, primarily about Goddesses, ancient rituals, and the ways in which patriarchal religions, primarily Christianity, have distorted or hidden the truth. Walker does not seek so

Atargatis

Princesse des Bâtons   Principessa di Bastoni
Princess of Wands
Prinzessin der Stäbe   Princesa de Bastos

Erda

Reine des Deniers   Regina di Denari
Queen of Pentacles
Königin der Pentakel   Reina de Oros

Baal

Roi des Deniers   Re di Denari
King of Pentacles
König der Pentakel   Rey de Oros

Galahad

Prince des Coupes   Principe di Coppe
Prince of Cups
Prinz der Kelche   Principe de Copas

much a woman-centered spirituality as a return to ancient mysteries of sexual union, as outlined in the Indian Goddess religion, Tantra, and the radical early Christians, the Gnostics.

Where the court cards in Motherpeace show ways of expressing spirituality, the court cards in Barbara Walker present Goddesses and Gods plus figures from the Grail stories.

The Princess of Wands is the Philistine Goddess, Atargatis, known in other places as Ishtar or Astarte. The Queen of Pentacles is Erda, the Earth. Walker does not explain the upside down pentacle over the Goddess's groin. The King of Pentacles is Baal, the mountain consort of the Middle Eastern Goddess (and therefore the mate of Atagartis). For each of these figures, as for all the other deities and rituals shown in the deck, Walker gives an historical account, and implications for our own understanding of such issues as religion, ecology, and sexuality. The book does not actually describe the

6

Les Amoureux   Gli Amanti
The Lovers
Die Liebenden   Los Enamorados

pictures themselves. Instead, it uses them as a springboard for information.

As a painter Walker is limited technically but with a dramatic flair and a sense of the wonders of mythology. In the Major Arcana she remains close to tradition, though with interesting alterations. In most older decks the Lovers shows a young man between two women, one dark, one light. People have assumed the card indicates a choice between temptations, or between good and evil. Walker suggests that one of the women is a priestess officiating at a wedding.

The Minor cards take familiar themes and recast them in imaginative scenes. She then uses these as springboards for discussions of various points of history. The Three of Pentacles gives her the opportunity to claim that the Runes, usually associated with Odin, came originally from the Triple Goddess, and were invented by women before the patriarchal takeover claimed them as masculine.

For the great majority of people, who have grown up believing that God is always male, and that human history began five thousand years ago, the information in the Barbara Walker Tarot will come as a surprise, even a liberation. Unfortunately, at least some of the specific details are suspect, while many of the 'facts' are actually theories.

Walker dismisses the usual connection of the Tarot's twenty-two trumps with the Kabbalah's twenty-two paths as coincidence. This may very well be so, but coincidence can also account for her own theory, that the Tarot comes from the twenty-one Taras of Tantra.

In her attempt to demonstrate that the

Tarot contained a heresy she describes the trumps as having been 'removed' and comments, 'The issue was a religious one.' She should know, however, that millions of people – mostly in Catholic countries – still play the game of Tarot, using the full deck, though without any esoteric symbols.

Like Vicki Noble, Walker treats modern Tarot designs as ancient. For the Three of cups she writes that 'three dancing female figures . . . continued to recall the older idea of the Graces as agents of kindly fate.' The image did not exist before the Rider Pack, published in 1910. (Notice the description of the card in the past tense.) At one point she claims that the Tarot is a thousand years old, whereas no historical evidence for it exists before the end of the fourteenth century.

Set against the problem of inaccuracy, we find Walker's ability to take an image and connect it to a web of meaning and information. The Four of Swords depicts a woman sitting in a cave. The text begins with the idea of 'Fatal Women', seeresses, sybils, and so on. It goes on to the Pythoness of

Delphi, Kali-worshipping yogis sitting cross-legged, a medieval ban on sitting cross-legged (a sign of witchcraft), Buddha sitting on the ground for the Earth to protect him, Antaeus and his fight with Heracles, and so on. Walker's pictures, sometimes lurd, often fantastic, can excite the imagination. Her book can open a world of information for us. If her version of the Tarot never existed in ancient times, we can thank Barbara Walker for inventing it.

New Amazon Tarot

Feminism, and especially the women's spirituality movement, greatly values the idea of the collective. Just as patriarchal cultures emphasize hierarchy, with a leader and followers, so women-centered societies encourage co-operation. Most Tarots come from one or

two creators, most often a single designer and a single artist. Both the New Amazon Tarot and the Daughters of the Moon Tarot (following) were conceived and developed by several women. The original group then sought artists to create the pictures. The

New Amazon deck begun as a project of Billie Potts, River Lightwomoon, and Susun S. Weed. Conflicts in the group led to Weed dropping out and eventually creating a deck of her own (see p. 123). For the art, the women solicited work from no less than twenty artists besides themselves. Techniques include pen and ink, photographs, photomontages, woodcuts, and papercuts. A number of cards show pen and ink versions of existing art objects. The objects come from individual artists, or from tribal sources. For the Crone (Death rather than the Hermit as in some other decks), Billie Potts has reproduced a processional puppet by Ellen Glanz, and set it in a vividly imagined background.

With such a variety of work we might expect a mixed level artistically. Some cards do tend to simplistic or sentimental images (such as, the Amazon of Wands or the Queen of Cups). The majority, however, are challenging, mysterious, and executed with skill and imagination. The Amazon of Swords, the Companion of Pentacles, and the Queen of Pentacles, present different concepts as well as styles, but each makes a strong statement.

The women allowed themselves, and therefore the artists, complete freedom in re-imagining the images. Billie Potts writes that they kept the Tarot framework because they believed that Tarot comes from matriarchal roots. The truth of this claim does not matter so much as it does with someone like Barbara Walker, for the New Amazon deck does not look to herstory for its primary justification.

Instead, Potts describes the cards as 'gateways opening in our collective and individual spirit passages'. They 'represent the seed-visions of spaces and relations still unseen, unknown, but imaged forth and in gestation now'. They seek a culture which is 'unseen' because non-existent in the world we know, yet 'imaged' by women with a belief in the transformative powers of the imagination. Therefore, the cards do not conform to any fixed ideas or symbolism, but only to the artist' own visions.

In a number of cases, two artists submitted pictures for a particular card. Rather than choosing one over the other, the deck includes both. Sometimes the two would vary greatly, as in Birth and the Horned One to replace the Devil. In the case of Art (Temperance) we might almost think the same artist had created both pictures. Both are pen and ink, with solid, strong lines. Both show art as developing out of the practicality of women's traditional work. In both cases, not only the work, but the women themselves merge with nature. A spider's web appears on the back of the weaver (by Kath). In the Potter (Jenna Weston) the standing woman's blanket merges with the landscape and the sky. Art is in the making, but also in the mystery, the face we see in the work, and the face that remains hidden.

People who use the deck for readings may worry about the double cards. We are twice as likely to draw Art as we are to draw the Crone, twice as likely to draw the Two of Cups as the Two of Swords. We cannot easily resolve this problem, but it helps when we realize that the cards are meant to inspire us, rather than give us fixed pieces of information.

In terms of traditional structure the greatest change comes in the court cards, which consist of Child, Amazon, Companion, and Queen. It seems odd to retain the last title, with its associations of feudalism (in her own deck Weed changes the last to Master.) The suit titles remain the same as in most modern decks (Ace of Wands, Two of Wands, etc). Many of the cards do not contain the suit emblem as part of the picture. Significantly, those which do keep the emblem tend toward weaker images. Compare the Five of Cups with the freer Nine of Swords, in which the lightning suggests faces in profile.

Many women have come to reject conventional standards of beauty as something imposed on them. They seek to honour women who are older, or heavier, or physically disabsled. The New Amazon deck includes such images as the Seven of Wands, the sun-dappled Innocents, and the Ace of Pentacles, which at least one woman I know considers her favourite card.

The New Amazon Tarot contains no images of men. While a deliberate decision, this policy does not seek to attack men, or to set them up as evil. Instead, the creators sought a positive deck, by and for women, one that will 'image forth' their own and other women's visions.

Daughters of the Moon

The Daughters of the Moon deck began as 'A Matriarchal Tarot', designed by Ffiona Morgan and Shekinah Mountainwater. At a certain point Shekinah Mountainwater left the project, and Ffiona Morgan redesigned the deck and the book that goes with it. The title page of the book reads 'All artwork visioned and designed by Ffiona Morgan.' It goes on to list ten artists.

The single designer gives the deck a more focused concept than the New Amazon Tarot. the fundamental purpose is similar. Morgan writes that her deck seeks to change 'ingrained basic beliefs' and 'retrain' women's 'minds and psyches'. Like Vicki Noble and Barbara Walker she wants to restore the past, especially that of 'the Great Goddess of ten-thousand names'. She refers to her deck as 'a Tarot of the "feminaries" ', using Monique Wittig's term for archives of 'wimmin's herstory'. The court cards and many other cards in the deck depict Goddesses from around the world.

Like many other women working with the Tarot, Morgan claims matriarchal roots for the cards. 'Many sources agree' she writes, that the Tarot replaced knowledge destroyed by the patriarchal takeover. She cites the often quoted idea of magicians from many countries meeting to create the cards. Besides the lack of any evidence for this legend, Morgan ignores the fact that those magicians are usually spoken of as men. Similarly, she says that 'Tarot has *always* been linked to the kabala, paganism, and witchcraft', ignoring Kabbala's extreme patriarchal history.

Matriarchal Tarot and Motherpeace both began at about the same time, and both took

years to complete. We can guess, therefore, that the idea of round cards occurred to Ffiona Morgan and Vicki Noble independently. Morgan considers the shape a way of overcoming either/or, right/wrong, upright/reversed duality. The cards become an image of the continuing cycle of day and night. They also suggest rituals performed by ancient women in stone circles.

As part of overcoming hierarchical ways of thinking, the deck does away with 'Major' and 'Minor' arcana, referring instead to five Arcana, one for each element, with Aether representing the trumps. The four material suits receive the names Flames (Wands), Cups, Blades (Swords), and Pentacles. Each of the four contains thirteen cards, a number sacred to Witches because of the thirteen months in the lunar year (the twelve months of the solar year are an arbitrary invention, for the sun only divides the year into quarters).

The 'court' cards become Maiden, Mother, Crone, the three aspects of the Triple Goddess. They are the three phases of the Moon, new, full, and old. They also signify the three distinct phases of a woman's life: before menstruation, fertility, and after menopause. The court cards all show different Goddesses. Each one connects that particular aspect to the element for the Arcana. Twelve court cards allows Daughters of the Moon to link each card to a zodiacal sign, without the clumsy extra cards in standard astrological

Tarots (see p. 136, Esoteric Tarots). Thus, the suit of Flames is Fire. The Maiden of Flames signifies Aries, the Mother Leo, and the Crone Sagittarius.

Like the New Amazon deck, the Daughters of the Moon is by and for women. It contains one male figure, Pan, as a replacement for the Devil. Morgan intends this card as a tribute to those men who are trying to change 'in positive ways by developing gentleness and self-love'.

Like other women's decks the cards honour images usually dismissed in contemporary culture. The Six of Pentacles shows children racing in wheelchairs. The Two of Flames, the Polynesian Goddess Mahuea, equates

creative power and fulfilment with great size.

The cards seem to me mixed artistically. Against such powerful pictures as the evocative Crone of Flames, or the Five of Flames, or the One of Blades, we find less imaginative or subtle cards, such as the Star, or Shakti, The Life Dancer.

A number of cards address issues of power, what it means for women, how they can achieve it and use it. At the same time, the deck often seems to try to tame power, to make the dangers of myth, as well as daily

life, safe and comfortable. Morgan writes of the Goddess Kali, 'Kali, the Awakener indicates only the necessary destruction for the creation of good.' But Kali is nothing if not excessive, longing for the ecstasy of dancing the universe to destruction. In creating positive images of wholeness, and nurturing, the cards somehow become drained of the strangeness, the occasional brutality, the ecstatic yearnings found in ancient myths and in living women.

A Poet's Tarot

Jesse Cougar has added words to the pictures of Tarot by including a poem on the back of each card. The style of both art and writing is simple and direct, though the drawings contain more subtlety and grace than the poetry.

The body of the Priestess has a realistic solidity. She stands against a background of

night and rolling hills, evoked in a few lines. The poem, 'Devotion', is a prayer: 'The bright moon's face/ shines from the surface/ of the water./ Such layers of reality/ are no illusion./ Goddess, I dedicate myself/ to reflect your love/ and shine with your power.'

The Six of Pens, which Cougar titles 'disc of roles' suggests the sweep of the Earth in the hawk's flight. The poem, however, is clumsy. 'Your riches are/ yours only/ for their sharing,/ and surely power belongs/ as much to the wind/ as to the hawk/ who rides it/ and uses it/ to her desire.' In the Thirteen of Pens, the stars seem to converge on the bat, while above we see the belly of the moon. The poem includes the lines,

'your cries are/ echoed back/ off many distant/ dreams.'

Cougar revives the ancient poetic practise, too often neglected, of creating new words. A pharon (replacing Death), taken from the Greek myth of the ferryman of the dead, is someone who helps others to cross over. The picture for this trump thirteen strikes me as doing very little with the concept. To replace the Moon, Cougar coins the word wildan, 'a woman in her wild state, our animal selves'.

For the suits Cougar suggests Sticks, Bowls, and Knives as alternate titles for Wands, Cups, and Swords. She then says that Pentacles 'evolved' into Pens, a nice image, especially for a deck including writing as well as pen and ink drawing.

Though Cougar declares herself a worshipper of the Goddess the deck is not mythological. Rather, it pursues the idea of creating possibilities for women to live different lives and create a different world. The Five of Knives shows a vegetable garden. Cougar does not shy away from pain, or pretend that women are always whole and helpful. The Six of Knives, titled 'blade of despair', shows scars on the woman's arm, implying self-inflicted wounds.

In general, Cougar draws scenes of nature with more assurance, and detail, than the human figures. The Twelve of Bowls is a nicely visualized image. The Ten of Sticks includes a sense of fantasy in the snaking branches. By contrast, the people in the Fool and the Magician are undeveloped. The idea in both cards develops the feminist recognition of different kinds of women. The Fool is deliberately drawn as not 'beautiful', with her large body, and the one shoulder out of line with the other. The Magician, titled 'Will', shows a woman in a wheelchair on a mountain-top.

Transparent Tarot/Goddesses of the Tarot

After leaving the New Amazon Tarot, Susun S. Weed devoted her energy to recovering and developing what she calls the 'Wise Woman' tradition, which philosophically refers to harmony with the Earth, and in practise means healing and life maintenance through herbal medicine.

In the early 1980s she began to work on her own Tarot drawings. At this point the deck is not finished, for she sees it as a slowly evolving project in the midst of her other work. However, she has prepared two pamphlets, one called Transparent Tarot, for the Minor Arcana, and the other Goddesses of the Tarot, for the trumps.

Weed's pictures employ varying styles, from the nearly abstract of the Ace of Swords, to the formal patterns of the Seven of Swords, to the realism of the Companion of Pentacles (the court cards are Master, Companion, Amazon, Child). The Three of Pentacles seems to show Maoist peasants.

Some artists realize their work more successfully by remaining simple. Weed's pictures succeed more when she stretches herself conceptually. Compare the delicate lines and layered reality of the Five of Pentacles with the somewhat cute Amazon of Cups.

The Transparent Tarot tries to show life lived by actual women rather than the idealized version found in some decks. The Two of Swords shows a woman smoking a cigarette and looking out the window. Weed refers to it as 'quiet but creative solitary thinking'. Weed's realism produces some images which many people will find harsh, even unacceptable. The Three of Swords is brutal and uncompromising, especially in contrast to the soft romanticism of some other women's Tarots. Weed describes it as 'A difficult decision, separation from a loved one, an unborn child, a dear home'. She goes on to say 'There is no escape from the profound sadness of life.' The card signifies a choice 'in your own interest, perhaps a choice which should be kept secret'.

The Five of Wands picture uses a combination of realism and abstraction to produce a sense of 'untameable, primal, fierce energy'. After a discussion of anger and pain in life, Weed ends with an astonishing statement. 'In association with the Fool, the Crone, or the Healer, this card indicates a need or ability to act from a deep sense of inner correctness, allowing you to kill swiftly and surely when the need arises.' Whether she means this literally or metaphorically it calls (at least) for some amplification.

The images for the Goddesses of the Tarot also vary in complexity and success. The Virgin (High Priestess) strikes me as too simplistic, especially compared to the daring figure of Strength, or the elegance of the Star. Weed has her say (the cards describe themselves), 'I

am the Virgin, owned by no man, irrational, untameable, savage and passionate.' This definition of virgin, as a free woman rather than a pre-sexual woman, is a strong example of women (re)claiming words for their own use. The Virgin takes many lovers, Weed tells us, while remaining 'pure and spotless, for her sexuality is not shameful but honourable'. The picture, unfortunately, does not convey either the power or the complexity of the idea.

The descriptions for the Major cards end with incantations based on the theme of calling the Goddess, both in the sense of summoning – 'Call me when the sun is high; I will come when the moon is full' – and naming – 'Call me Lilith. Call me Pythia. . .'. The level of writing in these prayers is inconsistent. At their best they point to a way of closeness with the image. The Star 'tells' us: 'I am distant and my thoughts turn in – call me persistently and often.'

CHAPTER 6
Psychological Tarots

This section contains Tarots which seek images which will act directly on mental states. Just as traditional esoteric Tarots try to express objective truths about the universe through a dancing woman, or an Emperor seated on his throne, so many people believe that we can express psychological conditions through pictures better than words. Words describe a situation; a picture objectifies it. Supposedly, a picture evoking happiness or sadness can become these things, rather than referring to them.

By extension, if we can objectify a certain condition, say, inner peace, if we can fix it on to a card as a picture, then by looking at the card we can produce the condition itself. This is partly the idea of the mandala, the complex geometrical diagrams used in meditation in Tibet and other places. In a certain way, all Tarots depend on this idea, except, of course, those used only to play the game of Tarock. Where mandalas and esoteric Tarots hope to induce mystical enlightenment, the psychological decks seek personal growth and renewal.

The decks range from the extremely complex Voyager Tarot to the deliberately plain Isis Tarot. The two seem very wide apart. In Isis we find such pictures as three birds flying, or a tree in winter. In Voyager we find Ken Knutson's elaborate collages, dense, breath-taking. Yet the two decks attempt a similar program – to move the mountain of the psyche with the lever of images. Though they may come at it from different directions,

both decks expect us to spend a long time looking at the pictures, Voyager because they contain so much, Isis because they contain so little. (I do not mean to place the two decks on a par artisitically, only to suggest that they serve a similar purpose.)

The Voyager Tarot follows the traditional structure of the deck, with twenty-two trumps and four suits of fourteen cards each. The designer, James Wanless, clearly loves structure, for his descriptions go deeply into relationships, between the parts, and within the Major Arcana (structural symbolism is a tradition in esoteric decks). The unfinished Kirwan Cards also stay close to traditional Tarot form, varying it in two significant ways. They include two extra cards, following a suggestion of Timothy Leary and Robert Anton Wilson. They also change the names of the suits to those of ordinary playing cards, such as Ace of Clubs, or Jack of Hearts. The Isis Tarot simplifies the structure, having twenty-two cards corresponding to the Major Arcana, and then another fourteen with no particular pattern. The Tarot of David Findlay follows a similar approach, while the Philosopher's Stone jettisons the entire Tarot form, consisting only of forty named and numbered cards, each one showing a particular state.

All these decks contain a sense that the old symbolism has become baggage. Even the Voyager, while keeping the outer forms, renews the contents, bringing together objects and scenes from myth, science, and daily life in the late twentieth century. The Kirwan Cards use such figures as scientists and bankers. Implicitly, the designers of these different decks trust that their own intuitions, their own sense of a certain image being right for a certain state, will apply as well to other people. They are gambling on the idea of a common humanity.

This approach brings us to a basic issue of re-imagination. At what point do we sacrifice too much when we do away with traditional forms? Can we truly find essential or universal images? Or do we end up the pictures that are trivial as well as personal? Even for those, like myself, who embrace the idea of re-imagining, these are questions not easily answered.

Voyager Tarot

Some people may find it surprising I did not include this deck with the Art Tarots. The collages, by Ken Knutson, with their deep colours and barrage of forms, display a sophistication and technique rare in this field where so much of the art is done by amateurs. I have placed it here because Knutson worked under the guidance of James Wanless, who sees the deck as a psychological tool for personal transformation. Like many people today, Wanless claims that we create our own reality, through our beliefs and expectations. Through visual symbols we can reach these deep levels of belief and modify them.

Now, this resembles the esoteric concept of the Tarot, which also seeks a transformation through symbols. There, however, the symbols come from a strict tradition. They belong to centuries of alchemy and Kabbalah, and are seen to reflect an objective structure for reality. This is different from Wanless's claim that we create reality ourselves. Where the esoteric view gives rigour, the psychological gives freedom. Wanless and Knutson

take for themselves the freedom to find/ choose the images they believe can help people change existence.

This does not mean that the deck lacks symbols. Wanless cites a system using animals, minerals, vegetables, elements, art, extraterrestrial worlds, along with domains of mind, body, spirit, heart, and collective unconscious. The decks' creators have drawn on nature and science, and Jungian psychology, but also on traditions of Tarot, Kabbalah, astrology, and myth. The choices, however, are primarily their own, rather than derived from a traditional teaching.

In contrast to the medieval style of traditional Tarots, or the archaic Goddesses and rituals of some women's decks, the Voyager Tarot embraces science and technology. The name for the deck comes from the Voyager spacecraft. Card twenty, titled Judgement in most decks (and showing the angel Gabriel with people rising from their tombs), becomes Time-Space. On the card of the Emperor we see New York skyscrapers and a picture of the Moon, as well as emblems of

wealth and power alongside the timelessness of nature. The Chariot includes an astronaut and a runway. The Sage of Crystals shows Einstein and astronomical photos.

Most commonly, the trump cards link mythic statues with scenes of plains, waterfalls, rivers. We see this in the Empress and the Hermit. The suit cards are more often a collection of objects and scenes suited to the theme, such as the musical instruments for 'Harmony', the Eight of Wands. The magnificent colours further develop the themes. In the Two of Cups, 'Equilibrium', deep blue dominates. In the Four, 'Anger', tones of red overpower shards of gold, blue, and green.

The back of the cards seem to portray a cosmic dance among the stars, with a figure in the centre like a skull, or a man sitting on a throne, surrounded by concentric rings of stick figures holding hands, the whole very much like Dante's vision of glory at the end

of the Divine Comedy. In fact, the picture shows a cross-section composite of DNA, the fundamental molecule of life.

Wanless explores the implications of the picture and the chemical itself. The ten points, or petals, suggest new cycles arising out of the completion of old ones. (This is one reason why the Wheel of Fortune is card ten in the Major Arcana.) Wanless sees the four suits of the Minor Arcana as 'defined' by DNA. The 'Attributes' of the suits are mind, emotion, body, spirit. For Wanless, mind has a crystal-like quality, and DNA is crystal-shaped, therefore Crystals replace Swords. Pentacles, the suit of matter and thus body, become Worlds because of DNA's spherical form. The flower shape of DNA gives flower images to the suit of Cups. And Wands symbolizes spirit due to the stars found in the molecule.

The court cards also derive from DNA, or at least the idea of genetic inheritance, for they signify generations. They are Man, Woman, Child, Sage (grandparent). The general descriptions of Man and Woman

strike me as clichéd and sexist. Women 'heal, nurture, protect, preserve', while Men are 'revolutionaries, transformers, [who] extend the frontiers of the world and of knowledge'. However, Wanless then describes the Woman

of Crystals as a figure of great will and mental power.

In some of his descriptions Wanless tends to a flowery style that hardly connects to people's lives. 'In your watery receptivity, you are the reflecting pool . . . Like the dolphin you tune in to others through vibrations.'

Some people may find the density of the collages difficult to enter. There is a flood of images, without the central person or action we know from conventional Tarots. Perhaps we need to go beyond the descriptions as well as our own knowledge and expectations of the Tarot, and instead explore the pictures.

The Philosopher's Stone

From the complex to the simple. From the dense collages of Ken Knutson to the stone heads of De Es Schwertberger. In alchemy the philosopher's stone grants immortality.

In these forty 'fortune-telling' cards De Es seeks to evoke fundamental states of being in the simplest possible images. There is an implied idea that patterns of stones, and

ERFOLG
REUSSITE
SUCCESS
30

URSPRUNG
ORIGINE
ORIGIN
33

stone faces, are more basic than other kinds of imagery. The deck begins with Order, and Self, the first showing a pattern of squares regressing into infinity, the second a glowing face. Later cards include such designs as Success, in which a final stone slots into an ordered pattern.

Of course, the sense of something basic is an illusion, for the images are sophisticated and witty. The card of Success implies that order and completion are more important than wealth or fame. But notice that all the other stones are cracked, so that this final one represents an achievement after many

represents an achievement after many attempts, perhaps even many lifetimes. Card 33, Origin, shows the land covered with pebbles pouring from a crack in a giant stone. The image reflects the mystical view of the universe as a single entity (pictured here as a stone, but in other places anything from a formless energy to a gigantic human being), which somehow became broken up into the isolated pieces we think of as reality.

Almost all the cards show either plain stones or heads. The only one to show a whole body is Existence, which depicts a man lifting a rock. It implies that life – exist-

28
BESTAND
EXISTENCE
EXISTENCE

MEISTERUNG
MAITRISE
MASTERSHIP
39

ence – is labour. With its suggestions of the
myth of Sisyphus it hints as well that labour
is futile. Several cards produce an ironic
tension between the title and the picture.
The penultimate card, Mastership, which De
Es describes as 'apogee, prime performance,
masterpiece', shows an incomplete image,
two halves of a mountain out of line with
each other. The final card bears the title
Solution, but it shows a question mark
before a blank wall. The sense of futility
becomes subtly changed when we notice that
the question casts a shadow of an exclamation
mark.

The heads recall Easter Island statues,
though without the square corners. De Es
often sets the cards in pairs. 6, Confrontation,

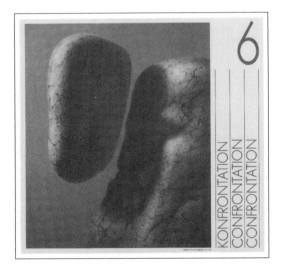

shows a large rock casting a shadow on a
frowning face. The next card, Breakthrough,
shows a similar rock split through the middle,
as if by concentration. Distance, 19, depicts
two identical faces pushing against a rock
which separates them. The act of trying to
come together holds up the barrier, which
would fall if they pulled back slightly. Card
20, Sharing, turns the heads around so that
the rock rests between them. They have not
solved their problems but have learned to

share them. And yet, harmony requires them
not to look at each other.

In contrast to the much grander Voyager
Tarot, the Philosopher's Stone makes it
easier to play with the images, to see (or create)
implications in the way they relate to each
other. De Es's method of reading the cards
follows a similar approach. He sets out a simple
five-card cross and then gives a long list of
suggestions on interpreting their relationships.

ENTFERNUNG
DISTANCE
DISTANCE 19

TEILEN
PARTAGER
SHARING 20

David Findlay

This set of cards bears no overall title, for it was painted privately by a London therapist to use in his work with clients, and for his own 'confrontation' with himself.

The deck consists of forty cards in two parts, I–XXI, and then again I–X, with card Nine in the second part missing. The ninth card consisted of a written account of a dream, but when Findlay photographed it, he found the words all ran together and so he discarded it from the deck.

The first part deals with 'finding a path through the personality', while the second concerns 'existential and transpersonal images and issues'. While we might think Findlay has based the set of twenty-one on the Tarot,

he actually compares the shorter series to the Major Arcana. The difference between the two sections is not extreme. The first contains such titles as Heart, Christ, and Desolation, while the second has titles like Tension, Illumination, and Surrender. Both feature a card called Out. The two cards imply psychic freedom. The first shows an astral body rising from a sleeper. In the second, a heavenly hand raises a ghostly figure from hands trying to hold him down. Findlay's comments for both cards involve death, though perhaps as a symbol. For Out 1 he writes 'even death is no escape from life', while he describes Out 2 as 'Life and death in my feelings'.

OUT XIII

OUT 2 VI

LOVE AND WILL III

The first section contains cards for Love and Will, perhaps as opposing forces, for Love shows Christ, while will, the following card, depicts a warrior. In part two they become united as Love and Will, a couple standing in a spotlight.

The style of drawing is plain and unpretentious, often cartoon-like. For the most part they accomplish what they set out to do. Some of the pictures are symbolic, such as Tension, and Mu. Others, like Will, or Dragon, use fantasy clichés. Some cards use a scene from daily life to concretize an abstract state. Pride shows someone drunk before a television, while above him we glimpse erotic paintings. Separation depicts a man, presumably in a bar, drinking one glass after another. At first we think of romantic separation, but then, when we see the chain fence beside him – and a gap revealing the stars – we realize that the card implies something more fundamental, the way modern life, and personal difficulties, separate us from the universe.

Isis Tarot

The box for the Isis Tarot describes the thirty-six pictures as 'psychecards', and 'an inner way to self-knowledge'. According to the information booklet, the artist Erna Droesbeke von Enge designed the cards through meditation. They attempt to show inner states in a direct way.

The first twenty-two cards derive from the Major Arcana. Instead of the usual figures and symbols von Enge has attempted to find images that will bring out the trump's essential quality, as if the esoteric symbols had grown on top of it. A few of these are mythological, and here the subject, if not the picture, remains close to tradition. Many decks interpret the Magician as Mercury, while we have seen how Egyptian symbolism connects Justice with the Goddess Ma'at.

A few others reduce the subject to geometry, as in Squares replacing the Emperor, or Triangle for 15, usually the Devil. Most, however, seek some naturalistic image. The Wheel of Fortune becomes simply the Wheel, rolling through a glowing light. Death becomes Winter, shown as a barren tree and grey clouds. Fourteen, which in traditional Tarot depicts an angel pouring water from one cup to another, here becomes Wave, as if we join with the water, rather than the concept of an angel.

The cards above 22 also display a mixture of styles and subjects. 23 is titled Energy.

1 Mercury

11 Maät

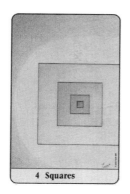

4 Squares

15 Triangle

10 The Wheel

13 Winter

14 Wave

23 Energy

24 Spinning Wheel

31 Harvest

34 Island

The snake and the apple suggest the biblical story, unusual in this deck which attempts to avoid references outside itself. By contrast, 24 shows a Spinning Wheel, leaving the interpretation to the viewer.

Most of the cards above 22 depict nature, usually something basic, such as Harvest or Island.

The small booklet for the deck gives 'State of Mind' and 'Oracle', hinting at a connection between mental states and seemingly external events. In a gentle way this points back to the Voyager, with its doctrine that we create our own reality.

Kirwan Cards

Like a number of other decks in this book, the Kirwan Cards are a work in progress, available to me as a number of sample cards with notes, the notes partly by Gary Ross of *Tarot Network News*. The San Francisco artist Kirwan sees the traditional Tarot as the 'Royal Road travelled by initiates of the gnostic path'. In his own deck, he seeks to 'build a new road toward understanding the human experience'. In other words, he hopes to broaden the Tarot to apply to ordinary people who do not know or care about esoteric religion. Instead of luring us into abstract or else mythological worlds, the Kirwan Cards attempt to trigger conversations with ourselves through showing us characters and scenes from our own lives.

This does not mean abandoning Tarot or its concepts. Gary Ross writes that Kirwan has taken 'great pains' to 'preserve the higher wisdom of the Tarot'. To bring the two levels together – higher wisdom and daily life – Kirwan has 'reunited' the Tarot with conventional playing cards. The cards are double-ended, like the face cards in a poker deck. Unlike poker cards, however, the two ends depict different pictures. The Jack of Clubs bears the title (not on the card) Artist/ Scientist. It shows two figures, both like the Greek God Apollo, one in daytime with quill pens, the other at night with a microscope.

Most of the cards differ more sharply at their two ends. The Three of Hearts shows

on one end a dark ball reflecting a rippling chessboard. The other side has a woman in a long dress dancing down a piano keyboard which stretches over the clouds to the sun.

For the trump cards Kirwan has done away with the usual symbolic names and figures. The titles refer to psychological states. Card 20 is Seeking/Finding. The picture depicts Seeking as a woman wrapped in a purple cloak and leafing through a large book. Elf-like people climb out of the book and over her body. When we turn the card over, Finding shows her having closed the book and thrown the cloak over it. She looks at the sunrise. The card makes a clear comment on the wisdom found in books, perhaps also on mythology.

The themes and some of the imagery correspond to traditional subjects. The Hierophant in most decks symbolizes wisdom and religious teachings. Kirwan makes this Wisdom/Comprehension. Through simple images he seeks to display the essence of the Hierophant in place of its usual doctrines. For IX, the Solitude half of Solitude/ Disquiet shows a fairly traditional Hermit holding up his lamp of truth.

The two ends of the cards tend to show either/or conditions. According to the notes the cards can help us overcome such dualities by showing us the 'connectives' between the sides. Some of the captions indicate how the opposites complement each other. 'Science structures art;/Art vitalizes science.' Others, however, imply a right and wrong approach. The Ace of Clubs is called Integrity/Delusion.

The King of Diamonds is Banker/Poet. Both sides display imaginative designs, the poet as a kind of Mt Rushmore Ernest Hemingway, the banker as a pinched face rising from a silver dollar. The caption tells us, 'The poet has roots in the earth./ The banker has liquidity.' With these images it becomes difficult to see how the banker represents something worthwhile.

To my knowledge these are the first cards deliberately to follow Timothy Leary's and Robert Anton Wilson's suggestion of two

more cards in the Major Arcana, to be numbered 00 and 000. According to *Tarot Network News* the two cards form a trilogy with the Fool. The three signify the Kabbalistic ideas of Ain, Ain Soph, and Ain Soph Aur. The notes for the Kirwan Tarot refer to them as 'the green slots in the red and black of our cosmic roulette wheel'. The samples available to me unfortunately did not include either of these cards. Nor did they include any of the 'Mistresses', the fourth face card to go with Jack, Queen, and King. This is a shame; the title suggests interesting possibilities.

CHAPTER 7
Esoteric Tarots

In a sense, Antoine Court de Gebelin invented the Tarot. When he declared the popular game of 'les Tarots' to be the long lost Book of Thoth he opened up a entire world of discoveries, speculations, absurd claims, and careful arguments that continues today. More important, he began a process leading to the use of images for meditation and spiritual development. In Court de Gebelin's time the game had already existed several hundred years, with no one really knowing its origin. Since then, as we have seen in this book, people have put forth many suggestions. Often they suggest them as fact, declaring with certainty that the Tarot comes from this or that ancient wisdom. On the other side, we find people insisting that the Tarot means nothing at all and never has. Against this last argument we might suggest a look at the Alchemical Tarot, the last deck in this book. Guido Gillabel's collection of prints demonstrates the remarkable closeness of Tarot images to those of alchemy.

Eliphas Lévi established the main line of occult interpretation with his link of Tarot with Kabbalah. In 1888 the Hermetic Order of the Golden Dawn elaborated and revised Lévi's system, further linking it to Rosicrucian, Masonic, Theosophical, and other ideas. The Golden Dawn produced a complex system of rituals, study, initiation – and Tarot. Since then, while people have modified the Golden Dawn method (for instance, some have returned to Lévi's order for the trumps) most occultists working with Tarot follow the Golden Dawn's approach as well as much of its symbolism. Of the decks included in this section, two, the Golden Dawn Tarot and the Hermetic Tarot, claim direct authority from the Order's teachings. A third, the Magickal Tarot, follows Aleister Crowley, a one-time member of the Golden Dawn. A fourth, the Tree of Life, bases its primary system on the Order. Yet another, the Mandala Astrological Tarot, actually presents the Golden Dawn's astrological correspondences without saying so directly. Various other decks, Gareth Knight, for instance, show the influence of the Order in such aspects as the names and imagery of the court cards.

As we have seen with such decks as Barbara Walker, or the Merlin Tarot, or the Haindl, the Tarot adapts very well to virtually any esoteric system. Previously, occultists argued over the true and absolute attributions of the cards. They would announce their vision as true and complete, with all others as false. Some of this tradition continues today. Elksinger names his deck the 'Perfected Tarot'. Others, however, take a looser view. Gareth Knight, a man truly learned in the Tarot's esoteric history and uses, advised each person to choose a deck which she or he considers 'congenial'. Knight suggests as well playing with the cards, and using them for fortune-telling, two practises once scorned by serious occultists.

For many years the Golden Dawn system remained secret, protected by the oaths of its members. As a result, some decks left out the actual information behind the symbolism. In recent years (some say as a mark of the coming Aquarian Age) occultists have opened up their secrets. Decks such as Tavaglione's Stairs of Gold display a staggering amount of information on every card. By contrast, Gareth Knight and Guido Gillabel have sought to simplify the pictures. Knight's cards, painted by Sander Littel, show conventional designs with very little adornment. Gillabel presents essential forms, often just a few lines or circles. Both seek to awaken particular responses deep in the psyche.

We have seen something of this idea before, that all images correspond to particular states, and that contemplating them, or working with them in some way, can evoke those states in the person. The occult view sees the universe as a structure emanating from God. This structure exists simultaneously in different dimensions, or worlds, including within each person. The Tree of Life describes this structure. Through studying the Tree, and meditating on it, we can learn to approach God. But the Tree is abstract, a set of ideas as much as images. Therefore, the Tarot has come into being as a lively pictorial version of the inner knowledge found on the Tree. In the Middle Ages, when most people could not read, many churches displayed a kind of comic strip of the gospels. For the Tarot Kabbalist the cards work in a similar way, leading us into the purer contemplation of the Tree itself.

No serious occultist believes people can transform themselves simply by looking at pictures. The process takes years of study and initiation. It also requires deep identification with the images. The Golden Dawn and other orders used the cards for learning and meditation, but also as outer forms of rituals. This last use, for some the most vital, becomes lost when the decks are simply sold on the open market. Still, the cards carry their own power. They can attract people who otherwise might never learn enough about esoteric ideas to discover that such things are worth investigating. One of my own favourite stories about the Tarot concerns Paul Foster Case, designer of a major esoteric deck and founder of the hermetic order, Builders of the Adytum. In his earlier years Case worked in vaudeville, knowing nothing of the occult. According to the legend, he was standing backstage one day, waiting to perform, when one of the other entertainers turned to him. 'Say, Case,' the man said, 'where do you suppose playing cards come from?'

A note on the Thoth Tarot of Aleister Crowley and Lady Frieda Harris

No survey of contemporary developments in Tarot would be complete without mentioning the new edition of the Thoth Tarot, designed by Aleister Crowley and painted by Lady Frieda Harris. The public first saw the cards as paintings, exhibited in London in 1942. For many years they were available only as the illustrations in Crowley's *The Book of Thoth*. Finally, in 1969, they were published as a deck, increasing their already important influence on new Tarots.

The 1969 edition contained somewhat weak colours. The new edition comes from fresh photographs and colour separations, producing clearer pictures, with more vivid colours. We can see Harris's surreal images, her complex use of form and structure, more as she meant us to see them. The deck also

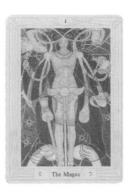

contains two 'new' cards, actually earlier versions of trump I, the Magus. Gary Ross, of *Tarot Network News*, has pointed out that the extra cards fulfil Leary's and Wilson's suggestion that the Major Arcana needs two more cards (see also Kirwan Cards). Whether or not we agree with this idea, the earlier forms of the Magus give us a greater knowledge of the art of Lady Frieda Harris.

Golden Dawn Tarot

In the Order of the Golden Dawn members were instructed to create their own decks, using as an example the original deck painted by Moina Mathers under the direction of her husband, MacGregor Mathers. Following this practice, Robert Wang has created a deck, using as a guide the deck of Israel Regardie. Regardie originally painted his cards while a member of the Stella Matutina, an offshoot of the original Order. Apparently, Regardie also worked from a copy. In his book *An Introduction to The Golden Dawn Tarot* Wang writes of the necessity to correct some details so as to make the deck as close to Mathers as possible.

Until the deck came out, in 1978, most occultists formed their impressions of the Tarot from the decks created by the Order's former members. A. E. Waite, Aleister Crowley, and Paul Foster Case had each instructed an artist in creating a deck. Each of those decks is complicated, with a great deal of symbolism, both in small details and in such things as the postures of the figures. If occultists expected something similar from Wang they must have been surprised. His cards, copying Mathers, contain simple pictures with far less symbolic content than we are used to from Crowley and the others.

The style is direct, with soft colours and gentle images, done by an artist who respects his own limitations. The Fool displays the deck's charm, while the Wheel of Fortune demonstrates a dreamlike quality, drawing us into its glowing center. Both lack the obvious symbolism we have come to expect, either coded into the picture, as in most versions of the Fool, or explicit, as in most Wheels, with their Egyptian Gods, Hebrew and Roman letters, Biblical beasts, and so on. Wang,

however, points out that this Wheel more clearly represents the zodiac than in other decks, for it contains twelves spokes, 'each in the proper colour derived from the Atziluth Paths of the Tree of Life' (see the Tree of Life Tarot, p. 143).

The Fool illustrates the differences between the various decks. The famous Waite-Smith version, a youth with a rose on a mountain-top, altered the traditional picture, that of a tramp attacked by a cat or a dog. The Golden Dawn version actually goes further from the original than Waite's later image. It shows an infant plucking a rose from a tree. What made Waite and then the others reject both the historical and the Golden Dawn examples? One standard answer is that they were protecting secrets which they had sworn not to reveal. But the picture of a babe and a flower hardly contains great secrets. The concealed treasures of the Golden Dawn lay more in its system and its doctrines than in Mathers's choice of images.

Some pictures were not followed up at all by later designs. Ever since the Waite-Smith deck appeared people have commented on the change Waite made in the card of the Lovers. Traditionally this showed a young man between two women. Waite changed this to a mature man and woman with an angel above them. Case's deck follows Waite very closely. Crowley's image is similar but more openly symbolic, showing the alchemical marriage of male and female, black and white. Without seeing the Golden Dawn version we might have supposed that the students took their ideas from the teacher. In fact, Mathers' Lovers shows a completely different scene, that of Perseus rescuing Andromeda. Wang cites this card as a much more exact representation of the theme of 'Divine Union, a mystery not even

2 THE HIGH PRIESTESS

3 THE EMPRESS

hinted at by the usual image'. I find this claim rather odd, for it seems to me that both the Waite and Crowley visions suggest Divine Union much more directly than the mythological scene.

Most of the cards seem simple compared to the ones we have come to know. The High Priestess is a pleasant picture, standing in pools of blue, with her Moon crown and her chalice. However, she lacks the connection to Kabbalist (or Masonic, or Theosophical) structures. She also loses the connection to the traditional Papess of the Tarot de Marseilles. Interestingly, the Empress appears before a curtain, the picture we usually associate with the High Priestess.

4 THE EMPEROR

5 THE HIEROPHANT

12 THE HANGED MAN

8 STRENGTH

Wang describes his deck as the first to reveal the true Golden Dawn secrets, without the deliberate deceptions of the earlier decks, whose creators feared such powerful infor-

mation falling into the wrong hands (as people used to say in old science fiction movies). He points out, for instance, that the Emperor places a foot on an actual ram, rather than having the symbol for Aries concealed in the throne. The Hierophant holds an open scroll, as if revealing the secrets to the initiate. With the deck published the secrets become revealed to the world. And yet, as Wang comments, 'the complexity occurs in the interpretation, not the picture.'

The deck is simple because the cards are meant for meditation. When a student had reached a certain level he or she learned to enter the world of the cards. This involved visualizing a mental image of the card and then stepping into it. The simple designs allowed easy visualization. In Wang's version, cards such as the Hanged Man, or Strength, have a capacity to draw us inwards. The one mythological trump, Perseus and Andromeda as the Lovers, has a childlike charm which gives it the feel of a fairy tale. And yet, one can do much more than Wang (Mathers) does with simple images.

The pip cards in the Minor suits tend to show the same scene on each one, with small variations. Hands emerge from clouds holding the symbols. In Cups, the water pouring or not pouring between the cups hints at different meanings. Swords play with the idea of a rose, sometimes visible, sometimes not, sometimes shown only as petals. The Aces are more elaborate than the other cards. They signify the 'root' of the element as well as the highest sephirah on the Tree of Life, that of Kether, the Crown. The Two of Cups includes dolphins, while the Two of Pentacles shows a snake curled into the sign for infinity. Notice that the pentacles are actually discs with a cross radiating twelve lines.
lines.

The court cards return to the style of the Major Arcana. The Kings all ride on horses, the Queens sit on thrones with elemental beasts as familiars. Beasts pull the Princes' chariots, while the bare-breasted Princesses all stand on their elements. The Queen of Swords holds a severed head. This, and other images from the Wang deck, also appear in various other Tarots.

One of the Golden Dawn's most famous

ACE OF WANDS

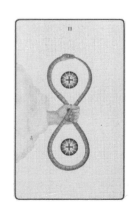

KING OF WANDS

QUEEN OF SWORDS

PRINCESS OF CUPS

PRINCE OF PENTACLES

innovations was new names for the court cards. The changes involved balancing the polarity of male and female. They also concerned assigning elements to each of the positions, so that a particular card became 'Air of Water', or 'Fire of Earth', and so on, depending on the person and the suit. For example, the King is fire and Pentacles is Earth, so that the King of Pentacles becomes Fire of Earth.

The cards also relate to the four letters of God's name in Hebrew. A problem comes with what to call the first male figure. The obvious choice is King, and that is what we see. But the element is Fire, which suggests a knight on horseback. The Golden Dawn employed an odd reversal in the naming. Wang gives the example of the suit of Wands. The Order refers to the King as 'The Lord of the Flame and the Lightning, King of the Spirit of Fire, KNIGHT OF WANDS.' It then describes the Prince as 'The Prince of the Chariot of Fire, KING OF WANDS.' Wang explains that the King begins as a Knight, marries the Queen and so becomes King. From their union comes the Prince, 'the New King.' The Princess remains apart from this story, for she symbolizes the 'recipient' of the qualities manifested in that suit. The system is an allegory, connecting the court cards to the process of creation described in the four-letter Name. It also links them to many ancient mythologies and rituals.

If we judge by the various decks the Order influenced, many people have found the titles unsatisfying. Waite kept the usual King, Queen, Knight, and Page, but hinted at a change with his reference to the Knight as older than the King. Crowley used Knight, Queen, Prince, and Princess, simplifying the allegory. The following deck, also claiming to base itself on the Golden Dawn, has King, Queen, Knight, and Princess, but refers to the Kings as 'Prince', and the Knights as 'Lord', an even more confusing arrangement, for then the Knights should have gone first, as in Crowley.

Wang's deck presents the Golden Dawn Tarot as it was meant to be – a personal copy of Moina Mathers' original paintings. Through his example, students once again can make their own versions (producing a copy of a copy of a copy). Through the books of Wang, Regardie, and others, they can acquire the details of the system. Unavoidably, they will miss perhaps the essential ingredient – the atmosphere, practises, and rituals of the Hermetic Order itself.

The Hermetic Tarot

Only one year after Wang published the Golden Dawn Tarot, Godfrey Dowson published the Hermetic Tarot, 'based upon the esoteric workings of the Secret Order of

Daughter of the Firmament

Spirit of the Mighty Waters

Magus of the Voice of Light

Lord of the Fire of the World

the Golden Dawn'. Despite some similar imagery the decks could not be more different. Where Wang (Mathers) is simple, Dowson is complicated. Where Wang's figures are plain and charming, Dowson's are distorted, even grotesque, such as the woman in the Star. Where Wang has stripped the deck of esoteric information and symbols, Dowson crams a great deal into each card, again as in the Star, or the Hanged Man.

There are certainly some elegant and graceful cards in the deck. The Hermit looks rather like a benevolent rabbi, while the Sun, one of the simplest in the deck, shows two dancing maidens in contrast to the usual boy and girl in a garden. Compare these, however, to the Princess of Cups, with her scarred looking body, stringy hair, and distorted animals.

The cards have both astrological symbols and angelic names worked into the pictures. Like many other decks the trumps display Hebrew letters along with the number at the top of each card. Other decks, such as the Golden Stairs (see p. 148) or the Egipcios Kier, actually contain more of this sort of information above the picture. Dowson, however, works the symbols more into the figures. The court cards display elemental signs at the top, so that the Princess of Cups, for instance, is clearly 'Earth of Water'. The signs are as follows: Fire, Water, Air, Earth. All cards bear the Golden Dawn title at the bottom, the Sun, for instance, being 'Lord of the Fire of the World'.

A number of cards, such as Justice or Temperance, contain several astrological signs. In Justice the sign for Libra is worked into

Princess of the Palace of the Floods

the design above the head, while Venus and Saturn appear more prominently in the scales. In Temperance, too, we need to look again to see the arrow of Saggitarius between the more prominent signs for Capricorn and Scorpio. Neither card really presents a problem, for the student can quickly learn the central symbol, and therefore see it as a mediating force between the other two.

More seriously, the deck assigns Pluto to the Foolish Man (Dowson's name for the Fool), and Uranus to The Last Judgement. This reverses the generally accepted attribution. Both these planets, plus Neptune, were not known at the time the Golden Dawn set up its system of astrological correspondence for the Tarot. As the booklet with the Hermetic Tarot describes, the trumps in the Golden Dawn consisted of twelve zodiac signs, seven planets, and three elements, Fire, Water, and Air, all of this experienced from the reality of the fourth element, Earth, which was not assigned to

Lord of Flame and Lightning

Queen of the Thrones of Waters

Lord of Dominion

Lord of Perfected Success

Lord of the Root of the Powers of Earth

any particular card. The discovery of the three outer planets greatly simplified the Major Arcana, for the additional three gave ten heavenly bodies and twelve signs, equalling twenty-two cards. (For more on this and other astrological information see the Tree of Life Tarot, below, and the Mandala Astrological Tarot, p. 152.)

The designs for the Minor cards also reflect the Golden Dawn astrological systems. The Knights, Queens, and Kings (Lords, Queens, Princes) of the four suits together make up the twelve signs. The Princesses signify the four elements. Similarly, in the numbered cards the Aces represent the elements, as well as the four quadrants of the North Pole. This leaves thirty-six cards, two through ten in each suit, to correspond to the 360 degrees of the zodiac. In other words, one card equals one 'decan', or 10 degrees. Each suit is an element, and each element contains three signs, so that a partic-ular sign stretches over three cards. Described briefly in this way, it sounds complicated and confusing. In practise the system works out neatly, even elegantly. The elegance, however, becomes lost in Dowson's cards, for the art tends to the same excess and distortion as the trumps.

Tree of Life Tarot

This Tarot, by Rufus Camphausen and Apolonia van Leeuwen, departs radically from virtually all previous designs. Many esoteric Tarots, especially those influenced by Eliphas Lévi and the later work of the golden Dawn, see the Tarot cards as linked to specific places on the Tree of Life. However, they have always found it valuable to put this information in symbolic form, shown as people in the trump and court cards, or arrangements of suit emblems in the Minor cards. The Tree of Life Tarot depicts the Tree itself, working from its most common form, the ten sephiroth, with the twenty-two pathways connecting them.

Before discussing the card we need to look briefly (very briefly, considering the vastness of the topic), at the construction

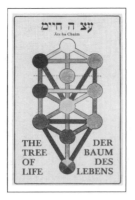

of the Tree, and therefore the deck.

The tree contains three triangles, the top one pointing up, and the other two pointing down. The tenth sephirah forms the root of the Tree. There is also an eleventh, or 'invisible' sephirah (we might define 'sephirah' as a circle, or a point, of emanation of God's light). This extra sephirah marks the barrier, or Abyss, dividing the three higher sephiroth, the 'supernals', from the seven lower ones. This barrier comes from our separateness from God, which the Kabbalist seeks to overcome.

There are, in fact, four trees, each one corresponding to one of the four worlds of creation. (According to Camphausen's book, *Mind Mirror*, the tradition of four Trees follows what he calls the 'School of Multiplication'. The 'Dividing Tradition' sees the four Worlds as parts of a single Tree. Multiplication clearly fits the Tarot, with its four suits.) These are the World of Archetypes (in

Hebrew, Atziluth), the World of Creation (Briah), the World of Formation (Yetzirah), and the World of Action (Assiah). The last corresponds to the physical universe (remember the Golden Dawn Wheel of Fortune, with its twelve spokes in the colours of Atziluth). The four Trees correspond to the four letters of God's name in Hebrew (traditional Jews refer to God as HaShem, which means The Name), the four elements, and therefore the four suits of the Tarot. Wands are Atziluth, Cups Briah, Swords Yetzirah, and Pentacles Assiah.

In the Tree of Life Tarot each suit has its own Tree, marked by different colours (red-Wands, blue-Cups, yellow-Swords, green-Pentacles), and the element sign at the top right corner. The number of the card becomes clear from the number of sephiroth coloured in on the tree.

Similarly the court cards show a progressive movement down the four letters of God's name. The King has one letter coloured in, the Princess four. Again, the colour and the sign at the top indicate the suit. Both progressions – the ten sephiroth and the four letters – depict the idea of creation, which Kabbalists describe both as a movement of God's energy down the Tree, and consisting of four steps, designated by the four letters. In a sense, the four-letter Name is not really a name at all, not in the sense of 'Rufus', or 'Rachel'. In scientific terminology, we can think of it as a formula of creation. Few decks show this so explicitly as the Tree of Life.

The Major Arcana corresponds to the paths connecting the sephiroth. The title card shows all the paths. Each trump presents the specific path appropriate to that card.

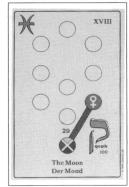

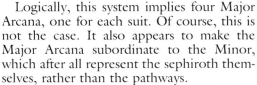

Logically, this system implies four Major Arcana, one for each suit. Of course, this is not the case. It also appears to make the Major Arcana subordinate to the Minor, which after all represent the sephiroth themselves, rather than the pathways.

At this point we should acknowledge that traditional Kabbalah does not recognize any connections to the Tarot. The links have all come from the other direction, from Tarot occultists exploring what seems an obvious correspondence. In his book Camphausen comments that some writers consider this correspondence 'pure coincidence'. He goes on to point out twenty-two paths on the Tree, twenty-two letters in the Hebrew alphabet (we could, of course, argue that the Kabbalists deliberately based the twenty-two paths on the twenty-two letters), twenty-two Tarot trumps, and an astrological system of ten heavenly bodies and twelve signs. 'I do not know,; Camphausen writes, 'which type of Brain/Mind one needs to maintain all of this as being co-incidental.' Still, the astrological connections did not work nearly so

smoothly before the discovery of Neptune, Uranus, and Pluto, and if two new planets really have appeared, the system becomes much more difficult to maintain. The same problem arises if we accept Leary's and Wilson's suggestion of two additional cards in the Major Arcana.

Not everyone will take to this deck. For some the diagrams will not convey feeling or awake the imagination. When I first saw them they struck me as 'flash cards' for occultists attempting to memorize the complex correspondences in Kabbalist Tarot. And yet, other people will respond to their rigour, their simplicity, their detailed information presented in the most direct way. I once brought several decks to a class I was teaching. When I passed them around one of the students became so entranced by the Tree of life Tarot he found it difficult to pay attention during the rest of the session. Having studied the deck, if even a little, I can see how wrong I was to dismiss it as no more than a study aid. There is a quality of essentials here. By showing the same structure on each card, with different parts lit up, the pictures show us the shifting forms and relationships between the cards. And the different lines do convey different meanings. If we compare the Priestess and the Empress, we can infer much about them from the contrast between the vertical and horizontal lines.

The progressive colouring in the Minor and court cards conveys the idea of manifestation as a progress through different stages. If we arrange the suit cards in the order Ace through Ten we get a hint of the world emerging from God's light. If we turn them around, however, beginning at the Ten, we see a picture of the Kabbalist's ancient longing to return from spiritual exile, a climb back up the tree to unity with God.

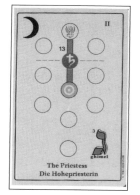

The Priestess
Die Hohepriesterin

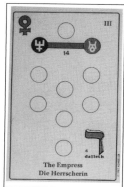

The Empress
Die Herrscherin

The Magickal Tarot

Anthony Clark originally created this deck for his own use, basing the ideas and correspondences primarily on Aleister Crowley, but also on sources such as John Dee and the *I Ching*. The cards are simpler and more accessible than the Crowley-Harris Tarot. While some people will miss the boldness and even grandeur of Lady Frieda Harris, others will find Clark's cards easier to use. Following the modern trend, Clark includes various pieces of information on the cards, such as astrological signs, Hebrew letters, angelic names in Hebrew, titles, such as 'Priestess of the Silver Star' for the High Priestess, and key words or descriptive phrases.

Clark follows Crowley's system fairly closely. Like Crowley he renames Justice as

Adjustment. However, he changes Crowley's card Lust (Strength in traditional decks) to Lust for Life, with a picture almost the opposite of the Thoth deck. He also keeps the names Art (Temperance), Aeon (Judgement) and Universe (World).

The Golden Dawn switched cards 8 and 11, making Strength 8 and Justice 11. Crowley kept them in their traditional places, but he gave them the Hebrew letters for places 8 and 11. In other words, in the Thoth Tarot Lust is 11, and Adjustment is 8, but they receive Hebrew letters 9 and 12 (the Fool, card 0, is Hebrew letter number 1, making the Magician 2, the High Priestess 3, and so on). This keeps the cards in their traditional order but rearranges the Hebrew alphabet, as if someone would recite the

English alphabet as A B C G E F D. Crowley did the same thing with the Emperor and the Star, keeping them in their usual places while switching their Hebrew letters. Clark follows Crowley on Adjustment and Lust For Life. With the Emperor and the Star, however, he does something even stranger. The Hebrew letters on the cards remain in their alphabetical order, with Heh in the corners of the Emperor, and Tzaddi in the corners and above the head of the Star maiden. However, to the left of the Emperor's head he writes in Roman letters the name 'tzaddi'. Is the Emperor Heh or Tzaddi? Someone wishing to use these cards Kabbalistically will find this very confusing.

The Major cards mostly show faces within geometric or other patterns. The Chariot has two sphinxes, both white, in contrast to the usual black and white to symbolize duality. The Tower, the Star, and the Moon show more elaborate pictures. Aeon displays the horoscope, while the Universe depicts the four Worlds of Kabbalah as Trees of Life converging on a central sphere which forms the bottom sephirah for each Tree.

The court cards show faces as well, some with scenes below or around the face. Elemental signs in the corners indicate the place in the system (such as Air of Earth, Water of Fire, and so on).

The suit cards contain English and Hebrew names, and the elemental sign in the corners. Most also display minature scenes, plus key words or phrases. The Ace of Disks demonstrates Clarkes's ability to draw delicate natural images.

Some of the capsule descriptions on the cards may seem extreme. For the Three of Swords we find 'Secrecy' and 'Perversion', while the Ten of Swords contains the phrase 'Reason divorced from reality'. We find the same excess in some of the comments in the booklet which accompanies the deck. For the Five of Disks Clark writes 'The head of a dog, such as may threaten sheep, signifies intelligence applied to labour.'

Enoil Gavat and Stairs of Gold

The work of Giorgio M. S. Tavaglione includes influences from Kabbalah, alchemy, Hinduism, Egyptian, Greek, and other mythology, Freemasonry, and the work of Dante Alighieri. His Tarots include the Oracle of Sibyl deck, which was not available to me,

and the two decks illustrated here, the Enoil Gavat and the Stairs of Gold. Judging from copyrights, the Enoil Gavat came first, with the Stairs of Gold, commissioned by Stuart Kaplan, further developing the ideas and imagery. Both decks are ornate, with gold

dominating the colouring. Enoil Gavat uses primarily Egyptian imagery, though the Fool, Hermit, Strength, and Star are more conventional.

The pictures for Stairs of Gold are medieval in style, and more elaborate, with developed backgrounds, as in the Chariot or the Tower. The court cards lack backgrounds, but contain much detail.

The elegance of the art is diminished by Tavaglione's tendency to portray all his women with large, pointed breasts, rather like the heroines in pornographic comic books.

Tavaglione has filled both decks with symbolic information, taken from many sources. We will look first at Enoil Gavat.

At the top left, on cards 1–9, we find a symbolic representation of the number. Top right for cards 1–10 shows a geometric form for the number. Top right for cards 11–21 show the number derived from the Hebrew letter for that card. In the row just below the top we find the Hebrew letter on the left, and a Sanskrit letter on the right. In the centre of the row, cards 2–7, plus 12 and 21, show an esoteric symbol (thus we see this on the High Priestess but not the Moon). Two-thirds down on the left we find the zodiacal or planetary glyph. Across from that appears the 'vulgar' Latin letter corresponding to the Hebrew and Sanskrit. In the centre, below the picture, we see the title of the card. Below that on cards 1–10 appears the name of the sephirah for that number from the Tree of Life. At the bottom we find key words for interpretation.

The actual picture in the centre of the card is said to have four levels, beginning with the formal, that is, the literal picture of a priestess, or an emperor, and so on. The second level is moral, teaching us a simple lesson. The third is allegorical, giving us the symbolic meanings. Finally we get to the anagogical, which means the divine sense, a non-intellectual realization of the card's mystery. These levels of meaning come from Dante (for comparison see the Dante Tarot p. 76). Tavaglione connects them as well to the four elements. The formal is Earth, the moral Water, the allegorical Air, the anagogical Fire. Notice that the system disrupts the Kabbalist order of the elements, which runs Earth, Air, Water, Fire.

The descriptions for the four suits follow the usual order more closely. Batons are described as Fire-yod (first letter of God's name)-Atzuluth-sulphur (alchemical substance). Cups are Water-heh-Briah-mercury. Swords are Air-vav-Yetzirah-nitrogen, and Coins-Earth-heh-Assiah-salt. A great deal of other information goes into the Minor cards as well, including winds, seasons, quarters of the Moon. Tavaglione also groups the numbers into four qualities. Knights, Nines, Eights, and Sevens signify the physical body, though Pages and Tens represent sexuality. Queens, sixes, fives, and fours, signify the life-force, while Kings, Threes, Twos, and Aces indicate intellect.

Tavaglione's Enoil Gavat demonstrates a desire to bring the whole world into the Tarot images. He carries this even further in the Stairs of Gold. The name comes from

Dante, canto XXI (fitting number) of the Paradiso. 'I saw a Stair the colour of gold on which shone a ray of Sun, which raised itself so high that my eyes could not see the top. . .' Gold is the alchemical symbol for perfection, and Tavaglione also compares the Tarot, and the spiritual quest, to a stepped pyramid, with a base of lead and an apex of gold. The descriptions of the cards draw on alchemy as well. The crossed legs of the Emperor are said to describe the sign for sulphur, which the Hanged Man then overturns, through purification by water. (This idea, like many others in the deck, is not original with Tavaglione, who is primarily a synthesist.) Freemasonry comes in with the symbol at the top of the title card and the

explicit identification of the Emperor with the 'Great Architect of Freemasonry'.

Once again we find the card decorated with Hebrew, Sanskrit, and Roman letters, with glyphs, numbers, geometric forms, key words, and so on. At the top left corner the box contains two symbols, the upper a letter in 'the Celestial Alphabet', the lower an esoteric symbol, such as the alchemical glyphs on the Emperor and the Hanged Man.

At the bottom left we find the particular path on the Tree of Life. When we look at the path for the Emperor we discover that Tavaglione has followed Crowley in assigning the card to path eighteen. In fact, The Tree follows Crowley throughout, and yet the Hebrew letters on the cards follow Eliphas Lévi, a completely different system, for it not only leaves the Emperor, the Star, Justice, and Strength in their traditional order, it also begins with the Magician as the first letter and therefore the first pathway. The Fool comes in between Judgement and the World. This means that for all cards other than the World the Hebrew letter at the top, and the Tree of Life pathway at the bottom, have nothing to do with each other.

Showing the two systems simultaneously allows people to keep them both in mind. Some, however, may find it confusing.

Tavaglione again describes four levels for

interpreting the pictures. In the individual card descriptions, however, he gives 'physical world, intellectual world, divine world', leaving out the moral, or perhaps the allegorical.

The descriptions for the trumps give mythological names and qualities for the people, such as this for the Emperor: 'Zeus, Jove, Serapis, the Sacred Bull Apis who after death becomes Osiris. . .' The names do not affect the pictures. In the court cards, we do not see mythological beings, though mythological names appear in the circle above the person's head, for all except the Pages. Notice that the name for the Knight of Swords is Diana, a Goddess.

As we might expect, a vast amount of information comes into the Minor suits,

some of it coded into the cards, some of it found in the booklet which comes with the deck. The designs for the suits are ornate.

The Stairs of Gold takes the idea of esoteric information about as far as we can imagine. If it all becomes overwhelming (and suspect, considering the confusion about the Tree of Life), the deck also gives us detailed and dramatic images. Death appears as a wild horseman, an image possibly borrowed from Waite-Smith but filled with movement and energy. In the card of the Moon we see the gate of a city. Since the road leads *out*, the scene takes place within civilization instead of in the wilderness. Fittingly, the dogs wear chains. And yet, the crayfish still emerges from the crack in the ground. In this picture we remember the ability of the *image* to lead us somewhere beyond all the formal systems.

Mandala Astrological Tarot

A great many Tarot decks include astrological information on at least the Major cards. Usually, though not always, the correspondences follow the Golden Dawn, changing it only to include the more modern discoveries of the outer planets. As we have seen, the Golden Dawn deck did not include glyphs or other written information on the cards. And most decks that do contain such signs sub-

ordinate them to the pictures.

A. T. Mann has created a deck dedicated to astrology. The system is primarily that of the Golden Dawn, though he does not state this in the book which accompanies the cards. (Stating the historical source would have made certain things clearer, such as the description of the trumps as twelve signs, seven planets, and three elements. This struc-

ture is not actually shown in the cards, which, like other modern decks, substitutes the outer planets for the three elements.) Each trump shows images essential to the inner meaning of the card, along with the planet or sign in the middle and related information on the sides. For instance, on the Fool we learn (at the bottom of the card) that it belongs to Uranus, and that Uranus rules Aquarius, and is exalted in Scorpio. On the Emperor we see that the trump belongs to Aries, which is ruled by Mars and exalted in the Sun.

In the court cards the glyphs become the dominant image. Along with the usual titles of King, Queen, Prince, Princess, Mann has added the names Crown, Throne, Chariot, Palace. They represent the three signs for that element, plus the element itself in the form of the Princess. This is the same system we have seen before.

The Minor cards show geometric forms created by the number of objects, with the relevant signs in the middle. Since three cards belong to each sign we learn which planet goes with each ten degrees. For instance, Cups 2, 3, and 4 are listed Moon Cancer, Pluto Cancer, Neptune Cancer. The Aces signify the element, linking the numbered cards to the Princesses, and thus

WAND KING

LEO   CROWN

CUP QUEEN

CANCER   THRONE

SWORD PRINCE

GEMINI   CHARIOT

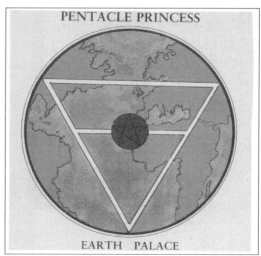

PENTACLE PRINCESS

EARTH   PALACE

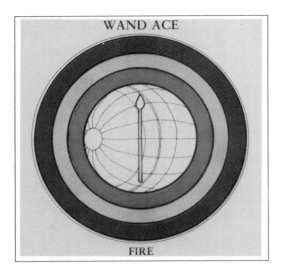

WAND ACE

FIRE

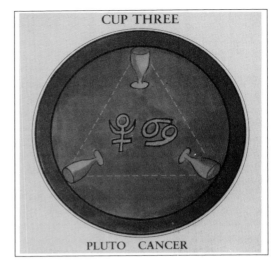

CUP THREE

PLUTO   CANCER

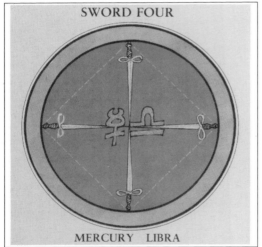

SWORD FOUR

MERCURY   LIBRA

PENTACLE NINE

SATURN   VIRGO

matching system for the court cards.

Mann maintains that the astrological symbols contain an objective power, that they affect the unconscious mind even when the person does not know their meanings. For myself I have always found this position difficult to accept, especially when we consider the variety of symbolic systems in the world (see, for instance, the Stairs of Gold, p. 148). Even if we accept the symbols as independent, Mann might have drawn them with more elegance and precision.

The Major cards do demonstrate more care and imagination. No people appear, but we do find the traditional symbols worked into colourful designs. In the Hermit the cloak and lantern hang on oppposite sides of a rainbow curtain. In the High Priest we see the keys overgrown with flowers. The Moon, which has always lacked people, comes closest to traditional design.

As with the round women's Tarots, the square shape takes us away from dualistic ideas. Mann gives a key to the positions in readings. Upright shows the person conscious of the quality of the card. Upside down shows the person unconscious of the quality. If the card falls with the title to the left it suggests the sunrise, and indicates that the person carries the quality in the personality

and will act it out. To the right indicates the quality derived from or projected on to other people.

Astrotaro

The 'standard' system of astrological correspondence for the Tarot is fairly simple, based on the obvious connection of twenty-two trumps with twelve signs and ten bodies, plus four suits for four elements. Astrology, however, is much more complicated than this, with such subjects as houses, aspects, nodes, ascendant and descendant, and so on. The Astrotaro, by Carol Herzer Abrams, explores some of these possibilities. Abrams

sees her work as 'theoretical and experimental', while based on a sound knowledge of astrology and a belief in the rightness of her own choices.

The last will pose a problem for some people, especially those who have worked with the Golden Dawn system. Abrams has made her own choices, for instance assigning Mercury to Strength, or Neptune to Temperance. We might criticize this as subjective, but we might also argue that the standard system is 'objective' primarily by common agreement. If we accept Abrams's system, then the Astrotaro can serve as a visual aid to the study of astrology, giving a concrete form to abstract formulas. For those who already know astrology the cards can help them see the planets and aspects in a fresh way. At the same time, they will not only need to accept Abrams's designations, they also will need to appreciate her lush and somewhat psychedelic style of art. The pictures, mostly abstract, come from her own sense of rightness rather than traditions of Tarot, astrology, or myth.

Abrams has produced two decks, one complete, the other a larger modified version of the trumps for use in meditation.

Abrams has added a twenty-third trump, Nemesis, to signify karma. This seemed to her a 'logical' step beyond card 13, which she connects to Pluto and the idea of collective unconscious. The complete deck also includes a title card which signifies the Lunar Nodes.

The full deck consists of ten planets, twelve houses, Nemesis, the lunar nodes, four elements and four Aces, twelve signs, and twelve aspects. Abrams began her work with the elements and Aces. When she studied astrology she painted pictures for the ten planets. As a practising astrologer she knew the importance of the twelve houses in casting a horoscope, and so she added these – rather than the signs – to round out the Major Arcana.

The aspects came in when she realized that the trumps formed complementary pairs if we set aside the Fool and the World. That is, 1 matches 11, 2 matches 12 and so on. Each pair then suggested a particular aspect, with the two single cards, the Fool and the World, joined to Semisextile and Quincunx. For example, the Magician (first trump, Third House), matches Strength of Mind (eleventh trump, Mercury). Together they belong to the aspect Conjunction.

The symbology, like the art in general, is personal and extravagant. Birds and jewels form the most constant images. Card 21, Heaven World, shows humanity united as a field of jewels. If Abrams begins with a naturalistic idea she often abstracts it. Card 9, Jupiter (Hermit) began with the image of a light on a mountain-top in Woodstock, New York, where Abrams lives. This suggested the Hermit with his lamp. In the picture the gleam of light becomes a minor image

beneath the Eastern meditation symbol. In fact, the original light came from a tv station in a near-by city, stirring a great many complaints in Woodstock and giving the artist a good reason to want to change it.

Many people will prefer to keep the more common system of attributions. Others will not care for Abrams's pictures. Nevertheless, the Astrotaro points the way to a fuller blending of Tarot with the intricacies of astrology.

The Masonic Tarot

Considering the importance of Freemasonry to occult tradition a Masonic Tarot seems long overdue. Through the Golden Dawn, and such decks as the Rider pack, many Masonic symbols have already found their way into Tarot tradition. The famous B and J on the High Priestess pillars in so many decks stand for Boaz and Jachin, the names on the pillars of the temple in ancient Jerusalem. But these names also form the passwords for the first and second degree of Masonic initiation. It is interesting that the letters do not appear in the Masonic Tarot.

Freemasonry is complex, with its own legends, primarily the murder of Hiram, Solomon's master architect. There is an intricate symbolism, much of it secret. All this ensures a deck difficult to understand without previous knowledge. In fact, the deck's creator, Jean Beauchard, emphasizes that neither the deck nor books on Freemasonry

can substitute for 'work in the lodges'. But this is not so different from other esoteric decks, especially those from earlier decades, when the Tarot served as an aid in rituals. And since the goal remains the same despite the system – a reunion of the self and the divine – even people ignorant of Freemasonry will understand much of what appears in the deck. And for those wishing to study it, the cards can help grasp the symbolism. Beauchard, of course, wishes to give more than information. He wants to entice us into Freemasonry itself. While some direct Masonic references appear in his text (in bold type), much remains hidden – not, he insists, to confuse or deceive, but to require the reader to 'discover' the truth through his or her own experience.

Unfortunately, the art is undeveloped, especially the representation of people.

If the designs are rough, they are also

lively. The trumps signify the basic story of
the Mason's initiation and development in
the craft. When Beauchard describes the
High Priestess as leading us inward we can
see it in the dark figure and the dramatic per-
spective. Images such as the snakes in the

Hermit or the embracing figures in the
Wheel of Fortune (notice the Kabbalist Tree
of Life behind the Wheel) can provoke the
imagination even without a full knowledge
of the intended meanings. And yet, the poor
technique weakens the effect.

Masonic symbolism involves 'rebuilding'
the destroyed Temple of Solomon. While
the Temple symbolizes mystic unity rather
than an actual building (recently, Christian
and Jewish fundamentalist groups have
plotted to blow up the Dome of the Rock in
Jerusalem and so pave the way for a third
temple), the theme of construction enters
into Masonic imagery. We see it, for
instance, in the tools on the Ace of Wands,
or the right angle and plumb line on the card

of the Lover. More subtly, Beauchard has
built each card on a geometric pattern. We
can see this in the Hierophant, with the
various pentacles, triangles, and interlocking
circles.

The text is often perplexing (another link
with older occult decks), but it also includes
some interesting suggestions, such as the
idea that the Lover signifies a choice
between intuition and study, mysticism and
gnosis.

El Gran Tarot Esoterico

Luis Pexa Longa has created this deck under the direction of Maritxu Guler, a man known in Spain as the 'White Witch, or Good Sorceror of Ulia', a mountain near San Sebastian. The publisher describes it as the 'first true and wholly Spanish Tarot in Europe'. The style is vigorous, based on woodcuts, with bold curves and braids used to show such things as hair, the sea, the fire.

There are many evocative pictures, not really explained in the short booklet. Why do we find the sea in Swords, when the Hebrew letter, Vav, indicates its usual designation as Air? In the Four of Swords we find a row of seven Moons across the surface of the water, with a crab, the lunar beast, beneath (the Ace has the sword piercing a crab). In the Seven of Swords we see the Moon in the sky, and the Sun beneath the water.

The deck contains Pagan influences, such as the stag horns on the Emperor, or the stag at the feet of the Hermit. We see both the Magician and the High Priestess in natural settings, without clothes. The High Priestess holds a pomegranate, identifying her with Persephone. In line with a European fortune-telling tradition the deck titles the two cards, El Consultant and La Consultants.

Some images connect to other esoteric decks, some not. In the Devil the caduceus

of Hermes (twined snakes around a staff) appears over the Devil's groin. We find a similar detail in the Stairs of Gold, with the explanation that it signifies dual sexuality. But the symbol means more than sexual energy, for it links the Devil to Hermes, to

healing, and to Apollo, God of rational restraint. Notice also in the card such details as the black Moon, the frog, and the hand signs of benediction. In the Wheel of Fortune the monkey comes from a long tradition. Guler and Longa give it an extra twist by having the crowned monkey hold a pinwheel. In the Sun we find the usual two children, but they sit apart from each other rather than holding hands, while above we see the marvellous Sun with its triple spiral of snakes. The colours – black, red, and green –

suggest alchemy. And what should we make of the Empress, with her bat wings, her ear of corn, and her shield with its dark triangle in the light of the Sun, and the white below, with the Moon and the night?

The court cards also contain suggestive images, such as the King of Wands standing on a burning lion, or the Queen of Swords on a lunar crescent at sea, or the Page of Pentacles balancing on a wheel.

The cards display Hebrew letters on the trumps, the court cards, and the Aces. The trumps also display astrological signs. Here Guler seems to have made his own choices, for he links the Empress to Mars, the Emperor to the Sun, Justice to Cancer, Strength to Venus, and so on. Without a clear explanation of this and other factors we cannot see this deck in the full esoteric sense, as a representation of a system. On an imaginative level, however, the deck can stimulate both feelings and ideas.

Gareth Knight Tarot

While some people, such as Giorgio Tavaglione, seek to cram more and more information onto every card, Gareth Knight – a Kabbalist, Hermetic magician, writer and teacher – has designed a deck that is deliberately simple, with a minimum of symbols. The artist, Sander Littel, has chosen a simplified style as well. While some of the pictures are interesting conceptually, such as Temperance, with its mixed day and night, or Death, with its jagged mountains, too many resemble the sort of quick cartoons seen on children's television.

Knight wishes to stimulate the imagintion so that people can use the cards for 'path-working', that is, travelling, in medition, through the twenty-two pathways on the Tree of Life. To do this, the pictures would need to evoke specific psychic states. To my taste (and as Knight stresses in his book, *The Treasure House of Images*, such things are very much a matter of taste) the pictures are too weak and amorphous to open up such inner doorways. The images

XIV TEMPERANCE

XI STRENGTH

IX THE HERMIT

IV THE EMPEROR

XVIII THE MOON

XVII THE STAR

VI THE LOVERS

work better when they become more detailed, such as the craggy face of the Emperor, or the rocky ground of the Moon, or the Star, where the water pours in four streams from the three-pronged tree. In the Lovers we see something like Barbara Walker's idea of the older woman as a priestess marrying the second woman to the man. The crowns and robes on the couple suggest the alchemical theme of the union of male and female within the self.

The court cards follow the Golden Dawn tradition of King, Queen, Prince, and Princess, with the Kings on horses, the Princes pulled by chariots, and so on. The Queen of Swords holds a severed head, the Princess a gorgon, both familiar to us from previous decks. The court cards show more imagination than most of the trumps. We see winged fish on the Prince of Cups, volcanoes and a leopard skin on the Queen of Wands.

| 1   ACE OF DISKS   1 | PRINCE OF CUPS | QUEEN OF WANDS | PRINCESS OF SWORDS |

Knight's book takes a balanced view of the Tarot and its history. Instead of announcing various legends as fact he refers to the Tarot's Renaissance origins. Instead of claiming the absolute correctness of one system over another, he advises people to choose a 'congenial deck and system', one which will open up their own meanings rather than indoctrinate them with someone else's. Knight describes the value of playing with the cards. Following a fantasy description in Charles Williams's novel *The Greater Trumps*, Knight suggests making cardboard supports for the

cards to stand upright. Setting up the images in particular patterns we can then imagine the images as alive and ourselves walking among them. Knight describes a method of setting out the Minor cards in a grand circle about the Fool, with the four suits symbolizing the seasons, the directions, and the four ages of humanity.

Knight's ideas are informative, his practical suggestions stimulating. The question remains whether many people will find the deck 'congenial'.

Tarok-Arcana Major Extensa

Danish artist Ole Christensen has created a modernized Tarot under the direction of Erwin Neutsky-Wulff. This 'extended' Major Arcana contains the twenty-two trumps plus eleven cards numbered 23–33, and showing mythological figures, some as simple designs, such as Horus, others more complex, such as

Lar, a figure reminiscent of the 'Venus' of Willendorf. Card twenty-two, Demeter, resembles a hippie bride, with her short skirt, her arm bands, and her necklace full of astrological symbols.

Some of the figures are comical, such as Larva, with her slit dress and her whip. Others

choose an image suggestive of the God rather than showing the expected figure. For Odin we see a dog instead of the deity on his eight-legged horse, or hanging from his tree. Christ becomes a chalice and flame.

The Major Arcana proper uses a variety of

images, some very modern, such as the scientist for the Magus, or the mushroom cloud for Judgement. There is a variety of styles here, from the complex Temperantia to the simple diagram of Augusta.

Some cards have interesting or witty variations of traditional meanings. Amatorii, the Lovers, shows a woman tied to a stake and staring in fear at something beyond the picture – perhaps us. The Hermit shows a contemporary man with a flashlight discovering the word 'religio' on a wall. He may have penetrated below the Earth to reach this revelation, or he may have believed he had reached a dead end.

The trump cards contain Hebrew letters along with their Danish equivalents. The suggestion of Kabbalah complements the Latin names. The extended cards contain letters and symbols. As a work of 'okkultisme

og magi' the cards lack some of the structure and complexity found in many esoteric decks. The pictures, however, are varied, humorous, and suggestive of ideas.

Elksinger's Perfected Tarot

Like Tavaglione, Elksinger brings together many influences and sources in his grandly named Perfected Tarot. The influences include alchemy, Kabbalah, Hinduism and Tibetan Buddhism, Robert Graves, Egyptian and North American religious traditions, and finally Neo-Paganism, with its emphasis on the divine in nature. Unlike Tavaglione, Elksinger does not simply display all of these as lists of symbols around the borders (though the tops of the cards do carry Hebrew letters, astrological signs, sometimes

alchemical symbols, and, in the Minor cards, the Latin names of plants and animals). Instead, he has synthesized his sources into the pictures themselves.

The art is mysterious and evocative, with a fine sense of detail. Such figures as Discriminator (Hierophant), and Champion (Chariot) lead us into a world of mythic intensity. The Minor cards are done clearly and with precision.

According to Elksinger's book the forms for the pictures came to him in meditation,

METAMORPHOSIS

TRIPLE MAGUS

PILGRIM

DOORKEEPER

along with a great deal of information about the cards. This included, for instance, the names of the Minor suits, Salamanders, Avians, Mariners, Terrestrials. While we might expect the Salamanders to show lizards, they in fact depict trees.

Whatever their source, various interesting ideas have found their way into the pictures. Metamorphosis depicts death as a man because of a link Elksinger makes between death and masculinity. Men, he argues, do not give life as mothers, they wage war, and finally, the penis 'dies' after ejaculation.

The deck has a certain male quality. In traditional Tarots the Fool appears as an androgynous boy, and the World as a woman described as hermaphrodite. Here,

both Pilgrim and Triple Magus are men, though the text describes the Triple Magus as 'the great androgyny'. And yet, certain male figures, such as Discriminator (shown above), appear very feminine. Doorkeeper (Emperor) looks somewhat like a woman wearing a false beard, in the manner of the woman Pharoah, Hatshepsut.

The deck uses alchemy as a mirror of the story told in the Major Arcana. The story concerns the Virgin (Magician) and his progress to the Triple Magus. Thus, Virgin is lead, Doorkeeper is tin, Fountainhead (High Priestess) Copper, and so on until Truth (Sun) as Gold and Triple Magus as Alchemic Gold.

VIRGIN

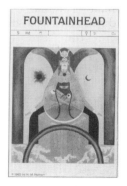

FOUNTAINHEAD

TRUTH

The Minor suits consist of fourteen cards, thirteen natural animals or plants, plus a mythological figure matching the suit.

The number thirteen links the cards to the months in the lunar year. In the Salamanders, Elksinger uses all North American plants,

but links them to the alphabet of the trees described by Robert Graves in *The White Goddess*. The idea for the Minor cards comes from a belief that 'spirit is always found inside solid forms'. It also comes from the Native American sense of kinship to all living

beings. Following the American tradition of transcendentalism, Elksinger maintains that if we examine life forms in their natural habitats we will perceive the reflections of our own spiritual, mental, and emotional being. The question remains, however, whether or not these cards will speak to people who have not spent time with the animals and plants in their natural settings.

Elksinger's book presents a great deal of information, much of it rather cryptic. An interesting theory of symbolism emerges in what he calls 'egregors'. These are symbols used again and again by different cultures, until the universe 'remembers' them (his quotation marks). In other words, they begin as something from individual and cultural imaginations, but eventually become part of external reality. Egregors, Elksinger maintains, can break through the 'membrane which imprisons the mind'. To this end, clearly, he has dedicated his deck.

The Tarots of Guido Gillabel

Like Osvaldo Menegazzi, Guido Gillabel works at producing a series of Tarot decks, each with a particular theme. Unlike Menegazzi, Gillabel does not see these as works of art, but rather psychic aids to spiritual liberation, the traditional aim of the esoteric Tarot. Included here are two decks Gillabel has drawn himself, both working from the simplest images, and one which he has assembled from the history of alchemical engravings.

Pictogram Tarot by Medicator

The first half of this deck uses glyphs and letters to convey the essential meanings of each trump. The second half, beginning with the Wheel, shows more naturalistic images. These too remain basic. The first three cards show letters. The O and I are traditional for the Fool and the Magician. In the N for the High Priestess the two vertical lines symbolize duality, with the diagonal line making each one a reverse of the other. N represents Negation, which becomes, in fact, an 'affirmation of what is denied'.

The deck then moves to an abstract serpent, a suggestion of the kundalini energy sometimes associated with the Empress. The up and down coils nicely signify the illusion of duality. Up and down appear opposite, but are part of the same curve. In card XV (the Devil) we again see a serpent, here coiled about the horns and pointing downwards to indicate matter.

Cards such as VI and IX show glyphs which none the less convey specific meanings. In IX the flame indicates the 'interior

Light of Man', while the four lines signify the elements. The picture actually resembles the Hanged Man more than the Hermit.

The natural images are, if anything, simpler than the glyphs. XIII shows rebirth as a flower growing from a skull. XVI, for the Tower, depicts the barest suggestion of lightning and shattered stone. And the lips of XXI, the last card, tell us 'After this, silence'.

The Cosmic Egg

Gillabel describes these cards as 'momentary meditative fragments'. Rather than claim absolute revelation for his work he describes the Tarot as a 'frame' around which we create a 'characteristic body', which I take to mean our own ideas and perceptions. We might also describe this body as the images we choose to put flesh around the skeleton of ideas.

The theme was inspired by Easter eggs, so that all the pictures work from ovals. The drawings are slightly more complex than the Pictograms, while still seeking an essential image. They also stay closer to conventional Tarot designs. The Tower shows a material Tower crumbling to reveal a spirit Tower beneath. The Moon shows a witch flying across the Moon. More radically, The Hanged

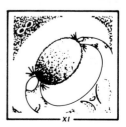

Man depicts the figure as a series of curves, while Strength conveys the idea of the card as a cosmic hand holding an egg (or an egg-shaped galaxy) without breaking the shell. Thus, Strength means delicacy as well as power.

The pictures can be playful or formal. The High Priestess creates the idea of non-ego through an ornate mirror poised between day and night. The Wheel of Fortune has the Tree of Life surrounded by the letters TARO and the signs for the four elements.

Alchemical Tarot by Hierophant

Many decks link the Tarot in some way with alchemy, for along with Kabbalah, alchemy forms the basis for much of Hermetic tradition. The Great Work of alchemy is the work of the Major Arcana – transformation, resolution of opposites, unity of the self with God. Quite a few decks show the alchemical crowned hermaphrodite for the card of the World. Instead of adapting alchemical ideas to a fresh set of images, Gillabel has gone to the extensive body of alchemical art, where he has found twenty-three images corresponding to the Tarot trumps. The closeness of so many of these pictures demonstrates the common sources of both traditions. For Strength we see a woman riding on a lioness, with cubs sucking at the beast's breasts. The chariot includes different coloured horses. Both of them resemble Chariot designs going back several centuries. In the Emperor we see him seated in profile, again a traditional Tarot form. He holds the same globe with cross we find in so many Tarot versions of the image. The cubic shape of his throne area belongs as well to the fourth trump.

As well as demonstrating links between traditions, the deck gives us a glimpse into the variety and magnificence of alchemical art. The pictures range from the fantastic realism of Strength (Michael Maier, 1617) to the almost modernist distortions of the Chariot (anonymous, fifteenth century). The latter picture shows Apollo and the nine Muses. The raven riding on Apollo's knee

symbolizes the nigredo, the step in alchemy in which the base metal breaks down.

The deck begins with a print of Mercury, God of alchemists as well as the trump of the Magician. The posture, with the raised arm and the bent leg, suggests the Hebrew letter aleph, attributed to the Magician before the Golden Dawn gave it to the Fool. Titled 'Spiritus Sulphur', it comes from 'Quinta Essentia', by Leonhart Thurneisser zum

Thurn, 1574. The deck ends with an extra card, titled simply 'The Alchemist', by Godfried Schulz, 1680.

Along the way we find many truly remarkable pictures, such as the Lover, an engraving from 1665 depicting the union of Hermes and Aphrodite, or the Empress, taken from a manuscript titled 'Actorum chymicorum holmiensium' and published in Stockholm in 1712. The picture seems inspired by the ancient statue of Artemis at Ephesus, one of the seven wonders of the world. The artist has added nipples to the round shapes, in the belief that they represent the multiple breasts of the Mother. Two days before I came to write this I happened to see a television program about the same statue. According to the presentor the very absence of nipples on the statue has suggested to archaeologists that the shapes are testicles, for many of the priests serving Artemis castrated themselves. The two lions on the Empress's shoulders signify her power. Gillabel points out that they suggest the Goddess Cybele, whose priests took the same drastic action as those of Artemis. Below her torso we see three levels, for the mineral, plant, and animal worlds. At the bottom Eros stokes the alchemical furnace with love.

The Alchemical Tarot forms a fitting end to this book, for it shows the way contemporary seekers unite the past with the present, re-imagining the Tarot in terms of its own ancient traditions. This is our Great Work, whether it emerges as art, or storytelling, or divination, or forms inspired out of dreams, or myth, or culture, or meditation. They come to us as images of a deep wisdom, and an even deeper longing.

Acknowledgements

Grateful acknowledgement is given to the following individuals and publishers for permission to reproduce pictures from their Tarot decks.

Ets J.M. Simon-France Cartes, 27, avenue Pierre-1er-de-Serbie-75116 Paris, France, for *Tarot de Louttre*, © 1981, Ets J.M. Simon; *Tarot Maddonni*, © 1981, Ets J.M. Simon; *Tarot Tzigane*, © 1984, Ets J.M. Simon; *Tarot Maconnique de Jean Beauchard*, © 1987, Ets. J.M. Simon.

Samuel Mercer, 6, rue du Mont-Thabor, F. 75001, Paris, France, for The Omaha Old Market Tarot, © Samuel Mercer.

Edizioni del Solleone di Vito Arienti, I-20035 Lissone (Mi. Italia), Via San Michele del Carso, 1, for *I Tarocchi di Valentina Visconti*, © 1982, Edizioni del Solleone; *Tarocco Storico del Palio di Pistoia*, © 1985, Edizioni del Solleone; *Omaggio A Erté*, © 1987, Edizioni del Solleone; *Solleone Tarot*, © 1981, Vito Arienti; *Future Solleone Tarot*, © 1987, Edizioni del Solleone; *Gli Arcani di Elisabetta*, © 1986, Edizioni del Solleone.

Il Meneghello di Osvaldo Menegazzi, Milano, Via Fara, 15, Italy, for *Tarocco delle Collezioni*, © 1979, Osvaldo Menegazzi; *Tarocco degli Animali*, © 1979, Osvaldo Menegazzi;

Le Calzature Fantastiche (special edition for Ricken, Denmark-Norway), © Osvaldo Menegazzi; *I Fiori Divinatori*, © 1980, Osvaldo Menegazzi; *22 Arcani Fumatori*, © Osvaldo Menegazzi; *Tobacco Tarot*, © 1980, Osvaldo Menegazzi; *Tarocco Della Musica*, © 1981, Osvaldo Menegazzi; *Le Mani Divinatori*, © 1979, Osvaldo Menegazzi; *Sardinia La Magia Nei Tarocchi*, © 1984, Osvaldo Menegazzi.

Droemersche Verlagsanstalt, Th. Knaur Nachf. Munchen, West Germany, for Der Haindl Tarot, © 1988, Droemersche Verlag.

Niki de St Phalle, for permission to photograph her Tarot statues in Garavicchio, Italy.

William J. Hurley and J.A. Horler, PO Box 194, Sausolito, CA, USA for The New Tarot Deck, © 1974, Wm. J. Hurley and J.A. Horler.

Carta Mundi NV, Visbeekstraat 22, 2300 Turnhout, Belgium for *The Simplified Tarot*, © 1984, Carta Mundi; *Tarot of Transition*, © 1983, Carta Mundi

US Games Systems, Inc., Stamford, CT 06902, USA, for *Rolla Nordic Tarot cards*, © 1980, US Games Systems, Inc.; *Tarot of the Witches cards*, © 1974, US Games Systems, Inc.; *Hanson-Roberts Tarot cards*, © 1984, US Games Systems, Inc.;

Sacred Rose Tarot cards, © 1982, US Games Systems, Inc.;
Tarot of the Cat People cards, © 1984, US Games Systems, Inc.;
Native American Tarot cards, © 1982, US Games Systems, Inc.;
Ravenswood Eastern Tarot cards, © 1980, US Games Systems, Inc.;
Ukiyoe Tarot cards, © 1982, US Games Systems, Inc.;
Egipcios Kier Tarot cards, © 1984, US Games Systems, Inc.;
Barbara Walker Tarot cards, © 1986, US Games Systems, Inc.;
Golden Dawn Tarot cards, © 1977, US Games Systems, Inc.;
Hermetic Tarot cards, © 1979, US Games Systems, Inc.;
Tavaglione Tarot cards, © 1980, US Games Systems, Inc.;
Gareth Knight Tarot cards, © 1984, US Games Systems, Inc.;
Secret Dakini Oracle deck, © 1977, US Games Systems, Inc.
Aleister Crowley Thoth Tarot deck, © 1987, Stuart Kaplan and Donald Weiser.
AGM Aktiengesellschaft Muller, PO Box 489, CH-8212 Neuhausen am Rheinfall, Switzerland, for
The Prager Tarot, © 1980, AGM Muller;
Neuzeit Tarot, © 1982, AGM Muller;
Zigeuner Tarot, © 1982, AGM Muller;
The Philosopher's Stone, © AGM Muller;
Tree-of-Life Tarot, © 1983, AGM Muller.
Aquarian Press, Thorsons Publishing Group, Wellingborough, Northamptonshire, England, for
Prediction Tarot, © 1985, Aquarian Press;
The Merlin Tarot, © 1988, Aquarian Press;
Norse Tarot, © 1989, Aquarian Press;
The Magickal Tarot, © 1986, Aquarian Press.
Eric Provoost, 47 rue de Bagnolet, Paris, France, for
The Minotarot, © 1982, Eric Provoost.
Arcana Publishing, PO Box 2, Wilmot, WI 53192, USA, for
The Xultun Tarot, © 1976, Peter Balin.
Earth Nation, PO Box 929, Nashville Indiana 47448, USA, for
Medicine Woman Tarot Deck, © Carol Bridges.
Ti Birchrose, Box 880523, Steamboat Plaza, CO 80488, for

The Celtic Tarot, © 1988, Ti Birchrose.
Heraclio Fournier, S.A., Apartado 94, 01080 Vitoria, Spain, for
Basque Mythical Tarot, © 1982, Heraclio Fournier;
El Gran Tarot Esoterico, © 1976, Heraclio Fournier.
Nicolaas van Beek, Amstelveenseweg 1090. 1081 JV Amsterdam, Netherlands, for
The Kashmir Tarot, © 1984, Nico van Beek.
Motherpeace, PO Box 1511, Cave Creek, AZ 85331, USA, for
Motherpeace Round Tarot, © 1981, 1982, Motherpeace.
Billie Potts, 18 Elm Street, Albany NY 12202, USA, for
New Amazon Tarot, © 1984, Billie Potts and River Lightwomoon;
Individual cards, © Carol Newhouse, Billie Potts, Ruth A. West, Tee Corinne, Liza Cowan, Kath, Paula Gottleib, Jenna Weston, Lizzie Brown, Ruth Mountaingrove.
Ffiona Morgan, 37155 Covelo Rd. Willits, CA 95490, USA, for
Daughters of the Moon Tarot, © 1984, 1986.
Tough Dove Book, PO Box 528, Little River, CA 95456, USA, for
A Poet's Tarot, © 1986, Jesse Cougar.
Susun S. Weed, PO Box 64, Woodstock NY 12498, USA, for
Transparent Tarot, © 1982, Susan S. Weed;
Goddesses of the Tarot, © 1983, Susan S. Weed.
Merrill-West Publishing, PO Box 1227, Carmel CA 93921, USA, for
Voyager Tarot, © 1984, James Wanless and Ken Knutson.
David Findlay, 2 Luid Street, St Johns, London SE 84JE, England, for
Findlay Cards, © 1987, David Findlay.
Uitgeverij Parsifal, Steenhouwersvest 57, B-2000 Antwerpen, Belgium, for
Isis Tarot, © 1985, Erna Droesbeke von Enge.
Kirwan, c/o 2860 California Street, San Francisco 94115, USA, for
Kirwan Cards, © 1988, Kirwan.
Altenburg-Stralsunder, PO Box 100352, D-7022 Leinfelden, West Germany, for
Enoil Gavat Tarot, © 1978, Giorgio Tavaglioni.

Acknowledgements 173

Macmillan London, Ltd., 4 Little Essex St.
London WC2R 3LF, England for
Mandala Astrological Tarot, © 1987, A.T.
  Mann.

Carol Herzer Abrams, 4 Broadview Road,
Woodstock, NY 12498, USA, for
Astrotaro, © 1986, 1987, Carol Herzer
  Abrams.

Borgen Forlag, Valbygaardsvej 33, DK-2500
Copenhagen, for
Tarok Arcana Majora Extensa, © 1987,
  Borgen.

H.M. Nelson, PO Box 3, 5712 Manor Road,
Austin Texas, 78723, USA, for
Elksinger's Perfected Tarot, © 1983, H.M.
  Nelson.

Gillabel Guido, 34, Steenweg op Heindonk,
2801 Heffen-Mechelen, Belgium, for
Pictogram Tarot, © 1987, Medicator;
Cosmic Egg Tarot, © 1987, Gillabel Guido;
Alchemisten Tarot, © 1987, Guido Gillabel.

Although every attempt has been made to
contact copyright holders of the various
Tarot decks in this book, we apologize for
any omissions.

Index of Tarots